RISK MANAGEMENT
FOR
PARK, RECREATION AND LEISURE SERVICES

JAMES A. PETERSON
Indiana University

MANAGEMENT LEARNING LABORATORIES, Ltd., Champaign, Illinois 61820

Published by   **Management Learning Laboratories, Ltd.**
                          501 S. Sixth St., P.O. Box M, Station A
                          Champaign, IL 61820

Design by   Neil & Lori Dawson -
                          Management Learning Laboratories, Ltd.

Printed by   Crouse Printing, Champaign, IL

Copyright   © **Management Learning Laboratories, Ltd.**
                          1987

Library of Congress Card No. 87-060135
ISBN 0-915611-05-8

TABLE OF CONTENTS

PREFACE

This manual is intended to be a basic primer in tort liability and negligence for persons working or studying in the park, recreation, and leisure services field either as paid professionals, volunteer leaders, university students, and/or citizen board and commission members.

The writer's purpose is to develop an awareness among leisure service providers to take the lead in managing risk within their organizations and to provide a method for offering quality leisure experiences with maximum protection for participants and adequate safeguards under the law for leaders, administrators, and the organizations offering the service.

The recent trend toward favorable treatment of the plaintiff (complaining party) and the obvious growth of tort liability in the leisure services field prompted the preparation of this manual.

The text is kept intentionally brief, simple, and as free of "legalese" as possible so that those untrained in the law may gain a healthy respect and appreciation for tort liability. Where cited, cases will be as current as possible, not that they are necessarily more important, but because they tend to show the present direction of the law.

With the overabundance of material available on the subject of tort liability, the writer approaches the subject with trepidation, humility, and perhaps a small qualm about the ideas and thoughts that he has appropriated and for which he cannot possibly give adequate credit. It is, however, with gratitude that the following individuals are recognized for their assistance and counsel in reading, criticizing, and recommending a variety of changes: Dr. Richard Lawson, Dr. W. Donald Martin, Don M. Jolley, Robert Goodrich, and D.L. Poer, Attorney at Law.

As a final caveat, this manual is not intended to offer legal advice; indeed the writer is not a lawyer. Users of this material are encouraged to consult legal and insurance counsel for advice when implementing a risk management program.

ACKNOWLEDGMENTS

The author is indebted to the following park and recreation departments, school districts, companies and associations who so graciously furnished material for the appendices: Suburban Hennepin Park District, Plymouth, MN; Bloomington Department of Parks and Recreation, Bloomington, IN; City of Kettering Parks and Recreation Department, Kettering, OH; Department of Parks, Recreation and Properties, Cleveland, OH; City of Woodstock, Recreation Division, Woodstock, IL; Johnson County Park and Recreation District, Shawnee Mission, KS; Jackson County Parks and Recreation, Blue Springs, MO; Department of Parks, Recreation and Public Lands, Billings, MT; Urbana Park District, Urbana, IL; Department of Parks and Recreation, Redmond, WA; Bensenville Park District, Bensenville, IL; Department of Parks and Recreation, Topeka, KS; Parks and Recreation Department, Sun Prairie, WI; Department of Parks and Recreation, Worthington, OH; Parks and Recreation Services Division, Eugene, OR; Park and Recreation Department, Cuyahoga Falls, OH; Parks and Recreation Board, Maple Grove, MN; Champaign Park District, Champaign, IL; Buffalo Grove Park District, Buffalo, IL; Niles Park District, Niles, IL; Miracle Recreation Equipment Co., Grinnell, IA; American Red Cross; Indiana Special Olympics; OSSEO Area Schools.

INTRODUCTION

Parks padlocked: Police patrol to keep kids out! Who would have thought a few years ago that city/county park and recreation systems throughout the country would be forced to close their operations? Who could have guessed that one reason would be the high cost of insurance premiums or, worse yet, the inability to find any coverage, no matter how great the cost?

Time magazine recently featured a cover story entitled "Sorry, Your Policy is Cancelled" (March 24, 1986). It referred to the problem as a new national crisis. The article goes on to say

> "Given the litigious nature of American society these days, just about any kind of business, profession or government agency is likely to become the target of a suit alleging malpractice or negligence resulting in personal injury. That makes liability insurance, the kind that pays off on such claims, just about as vital as oil in keeping the economy functioning. But in the past two years, liability insurance has become the kind of resource that oil was in the 1970s: prohibitively expensive, when it can be bought at all."

The result is that hundreds of communities are doing what the insurance industry calls "going bare" or becoming "self insured", which means that the governmental unit involved would pay for any judgement rendered against it. It is a form of municipal Russian roulette.

The cost of this national crisis is shocking. In 1985 approximately 9.1 billion dollars was paid in liability insurance premiums. In perspective, this is equal to the combined 1985 budgets of the National Aeronautics and Space Administration and the Central Intelligence Agency. The next total outlay for liability premiums will indeed be staggering.

The blame for the abrupt changes is difficult to assess. Certainly the insurance industry must share some of the blame due to poor fiscal management in the late 1970s and early 1980s. In 1984 the industry faced its first loss since the 1906 San Francisco earthquake. It was thrown into panic increases to make up for less-than-prudent management practices.

It also is no secret that individuals are more than ever unwilling to accept responsibility for their own actions and are turning to the courts for relief. The courts on the other hand are moving away from determining who is at fault in favor of who can best afford to pay, regardless of who was at fault.

There is little question that the insurance industry and the tort system must share the blame for the present situation in which recreation service providers find themselves. Some reforms within the insurance industry and within the tort liability system are necessary. Such reforms will not happen overnight.

In the meantime, it is essential to develop alternative methods to reduce the risks associated with providing recreation services. No one in the system is immune from litigation: everyone from the custodian to president of the board has some responsibility. Legal involvements are very costly and time consuming. A good risk management plan should be designed first and foremost to allow participants a quality experience in safe surroundings. The plan should also include provisions to protect the service providers from undue risk. In the words of Betty van der Smissen, "A basic, systematic risk management program must be instituted in order to minimize the likelihood of injury, and hence being sued; but if one is sued then such a plan can assist greatly in the defense. The policy-making body of the corporate entity should establish a 'risk policy' and then implementing procedures should be developed."

• What can be done?

• How can you become a part of the process?

This manual and supplemental workbooks will increase your understanding of the subject and provide practical opportunities and situations directed toward a better understanding of tort liability and the essentials for managing risk.

Legal scholars have been trying to define the word "tort" for more than a hundred years with the admission that a really satisfactory definition is yet to be found.[1]

Tort is derived from the Latin "Tortus," which means twisted or distorted. Good oldWebster says a tort is "A wrongful act for which a civil action will lie (take place) except one involving a breach of contract: a civil wrong independent of a contract."[2] Prosser and Keeton point out that "Broadly speaking, a tort is a civil wrong, other than a breach of contract, for which the court will provide a remedy in the form of an action for damages."[3] However, in the same breath, Prosser and Keeton suggest that this vague statement is inaccurate and then use six pages of copy to define what torts are.

What can we do as novice readers of the law? We can leave the scholarly arguments to those better equipped to handle them and accept that for our purposes a tort is a civil wrong independent of a contract that leads to personal injury or damage to property.

DIFFERENCE BETWEEN A TORT (CIVIL WRONG) AND A CRIME

A crime is an offense against the public at large providing a penalty against the offender. Criminal prosecution by the state is designed to protect and vindicate the interests of the public as a whole. This is done by making the criminal "pay" through fines, imprisonment, or in some cases death. "A criminal prosecution is not concerned directly with compensation of the injured individual against whom the crime is committed, and the victim's only formal part in it is that of an accuser and a witness for the state. So far as the criminal law is concerned, the victim will leave the courtroom empty handed."[4]

On the other hand, a civil action for a tort is initiated and carried on by the injured person (plaintiff) with the idea of being compensated for damages suffered at the expense of the wrongdoer (defendant). If the plaintiffs are successful, they may receive a sum of money enforceable against the defendant.

Tort law can include many types of actions, such as battery, assault, false imprisonment, defamation, trespass to land, trespass to chattels (property other than real estate), conversion (dealing with property of another without right), invasion of privacy, and of course, negligent behavior. This latter element of tort law, negligence, will be the focus of this manual.

ELEMENTS OF TORT ACTIONS

Three elements must be present before a given act may be considered tortious.

1. A breach of a legal duty that requires a person to conform to a certain standard to prevent injury.
2. Some causal connection between the legal duty and the resulting injury.
3. Actual loss or damage to the person or property of another.

1

A WORD ABOUT CONTRACT LIABILITY

Ronald A. Kaiser succinctly summarizes the prudent administrator's role in contract administration when he says they should consider the following basic points:

Authorization.. Check with legal counsel to ascertain statutory and municipal charter of ordinance authorization for the contract contemplated.

Contract Terms. Prior to entering into contract negotiations, the administrator should compile a list of nonnegotiable and negotiable contract requirements. These requirements, along with compensation, contract time periods, and contract parties, should be clearly identified. Contracts that are ambiguous and lack detail are invitations to a breach and litigation. The administrator should be guided by the rule that the contract must be of sufficient detail to guarantee the level of service contemplated within a reasonable time period and for adequate consideration. Unrealistic terms and criteria lead to problems. Incorporate all terms into the written document.

Bidding. Public agencies generally are required to seek bids on certain types of contracts or on contracts above certain dollar values. This procedure is governed by state statute as well as local procedures and ordinances. A prudent administrator should determine bid requirements and specifications prior to negotiating any contract. Frequently, nonprofit recreation agencies, as a matter of corporate policy, seek bids on selected purchases. These procedures are not as elaborate as the public bid process.

Contract Review. An administrator should develop policies and procedures for reviewing contracts with a legal counsel. The key to successful contract reviews is in establishing and adhering to policy and procedure.

Contract law is a very complex area of law, and the advice of legal counsel should be part of contract considerations. Attorneys should not make management and budget-related decisions on contracts but should assist the administrator in preparing a contract document that is unambiguous and meets the goals sought by the parties."[5]

While we recognize the importance of contract liability to the park, recreation, and leisure services field, it is too broad a subject to be included in any detail in this manual.

SOVEREIGN IMMUNITY

"An immunity is a freedom from suit or liability"[6]

Historically, federal and state governments, as well as cities and towns, were immune from tort liability arising from activities that were governmental in nature. "Most jurisdictions, however, have abandoned this doctrine in favor of permitting tort actions with certain limitations and restrictions."[7]

FEDERAL TORT CLAIMS ACT "The government of the United States may not be sued in tort without its consent. That consent was given in the Federal Tort Claims Act (FTCA, 1946), which largely abolished the federal government's immunity from tort liability and established the conditions for suits and claims against the federal government."[8]

STATE AND LOCAL AGENCIES   Even though two states (Maryland and Mississippi) have retained something close to total sovereign immunity, the vast majority of states has consented to some liability for torts.

"The most striking feature of the tort law of governmental entities today is that the immunities, once almost total, have been largely abolished or severely restricted at almost all levels -- to a large extent it appears that the change will continue, and the day may be at hand when the immunity as traditionally known no longer represents the first line of defense for governmental units."[9] That day is here.

RECREATION USE STATUTES   There is a relatively new form of limited immunity called recreation use statutes. It was originally developed for private landowners but it does apply in some form to federal and state jurisdictions. The Council of State Governments developed a "model" of the legislation in 1965, and some form of the model has been adopted by 47 jurisdictions to date. Those not included at this time are Alaska, Mississippi, Missouri, and the District of Columbia. According to James C. Kozlowski:

"Under a recreational use statute, the landowner owes no duty of care to recreational users to guard or warn against known or discoverable hazards on the premises. This statutory immunity is lost, however, where a fee is charged for the use of the premises or the landowner is guilty of willful or wanton misconduct. Unlike mere carelessness constituting negligence, willful/wanton misconduct is more outrageous behavior demonstrating an utter disregard for the physical well being of others."[10]

Kozlowski says that "under the Federal Torts Claims Act (FTCA), the federal government is held liable like a private individual under the law of the jurisdiction where the injury occurred."[11] This means that the federal government is provided protection similar to that accorded private landowners under terms of the FTCA.

However, unlike the federal courts, state courts have been slow to determine if these recreational use statutes apply to state and local government. "At this point in time, state courts in approximately 19 jurisdictions have considered the applicability of the state recreational use statute to the state and local governments."[12]

PRIVATE AND QUASI-PRIVATE AGENCIES   Private corporations such as racquetball or tennis clubs or agencies such as the YMCA or Boys Club are not governmental in nature and are not offered immunity from liability. However, the doctrine of respondeat superior does apply: this means that the corporation, business, or agency may be liable for the tortious acts of its trustees, officers, and employees.

RESPONDEAT SUPERIOR AND ULTRA VIRES ACT

The doctrine of respondeat superior has broad implications to the park, recreation, and leisure

services field, for board and commissioner members, for administrative officers, and for leaders, teachers, coaches, and volunteers.

The doctrine of respondeat superior (let the master answer) means that the municipality or corporation is liable in certain cases for the wrongful acts of its employees as long as they are performing within the scope of their responsibilities. [An] "*ultra vires act* [beyond the scope of duty] of [a] municipality is one which is beyond powers conferred upon it by law [state statute]."[13] "Such acts beyond the scope of powers of a corporation [private, quasi-private] are defined by the [corporation's] charter or laws of state incorporation."[14]

If this sounds a little like an unusual language, don't despair! In more simple words it tells us that the agency for which we work is responsible for our actions, in most cases, as long as we are working within the scope of out assigned responsibilities. Everyone in the work chain must know and act within the limits of their prescribed duties. As long as they do, they will enjoy certain protections under the law. It is extremely important, therefore, that everyone from board members to volunteers has a clear understanding of their duties. What's the best way to accomplish that? Job descriptions. Are yours up to date?

WHO IS LIABLE?

SPONSORS, OWNERS, BOARDS OF DIRECTORS   Are park and recreation board and commission members, owners and program sponsors liable?

As a general rule, members of boards and commissions, as well as officers of private recreation agencies, whether elected or appointed, are not personally liable for their actions as long as they are acting within the scope of their authority. They are not liable for their employees who may commit negligent acts unless they are party to the act.

ADMINISTRATORS AND SUPERVISORS   Essentially, administrators and supervisors are liable for their own acts of negligence just like any individual or employee. Administrative officers such as superintendents, directors, managers, supervisors, etc., are not responsible for negligent acts of their subordinates when that liability is based on supervisory responsibility. Otherwise it would be impossible to fill such positions. There are two exceptions:

1. If the administrator and/or supervisor participated in or in any way directed, ratified, or condoned the negligent act of an employee, the administrator may be liable.

2. Administrators and supervisors may be liable for:

    a. Incompetent hiring practices
    b. Failure to recognize necessity for firing
    c. Inadequate documentation of firing
    d. Inaccurate or incomplete job descriptions
    e. Insufficient training of staff
    f. Unclear establishment and/or enforcement of safety rules and regulations
    g. Failure to study and comply with statutory and/or corporation requirements
    h. Failure to remedy dangerous conditions
    i. Failure to give notice to others of known unsafe conditions

g. Failure to study and comply with statutory and/or corporation requirements
h. Failure to remedy dangerous conditions
i. Failure to give notice to others of known unsafe conditions

LEADERS, TEACHERS, COACHES, VOLUNTEERS   When may leaders, teachers, coaches, and volunteers be liable?

What little governmental immunity that remains does not cover individual leaders, teachers, coaches, or volunteers. Consequently, both public and private employees may be liable for tortious conduct and can be sued under most circumstances any time.

In most states indemnification (hold harmless) provisions have been passed in the form of tort claim acts to protect public employees. Most tort claims acts provide for legal counsel for the employee and will pay for damages awarded, usually with some limits regarding the total award. Indemnification implies that the employee was acting within the scope of duties (not an ultra vires act) at the time of the accident, and that it was not of a willful or wanton nature. Since these provisions vary by state, readers are encouraged to seek legal advice regarding their states' provisions.

Special attention is drawn to the volunteers because park, recreation, and leisure service agencies make extensive use of volunteers in a variety of roles. While their time and effort is not recognized with monetary rewards, each supervisor should consider them as members of the staff in terms of a written job description, schedule of duty, training responsibilities, and so forth. Each volunteer is responsible for his own negligent acts. In addition, volunteers may well subject the agency to liability for their negligence. It behooves all park, recreation, and leisure services agencies to be extremely careful in recruiting, selecting, training, and supervising volunteers.

SUMMARY   Who is liable? Under certain circumstances, everyone is. The board, administrators, supervisors, leaders, and volunteers are subjected to varying degrees of liability. The key for administrators of park, recreation, and leisure service agencies is to:

- Know your statutory duties (state laws) or charter duties (private, quasi-private agencies).

- Make certain that your board, employees, and volunteers are briefed on their responsibilities.

- Develop adequate recruiting, selecting, training, and supervisory procedures.

- Establish rules and regulations; see that they are enforced.

- Have written job descriptions.

- Know your state's indemnification laws.

- Develop a comprehensive risk management plan.

NOTES CHAPTER I

1. W. Prosser and W. Keeton, The Law of Torts, 5th. ed. (St. Paul: West Publishing Co., 1985) p. 1.

2. Webster's Third International Dictionary (1981).

3. Prosser and Keeton, p. 2.

4. Id. at p. 7.

5. Ronald A. Kaiser, Liability and Law in Recreation, Parks, and Sports (1986), p. 40 Reprinted by permission of Prentice-Hall, Inc., Englewood Cliffs, New Jersey.

6. Prosser and Keeton, p. 1032.

7. Black's Law Dictionary, p. 1252 (5th. ed. 1979).

8. Id. at p. 552.

9. Prosser and Keeton, pp. 1055-1056.

10. James C. Kozlowski, Recreational Use Law Applies to Public Land in NY, NE, ID, OH, and WA. Parks and Recreation, Oct., 1986, p. 22.

11. Id. at p. 22.

12. Id. at p. 24.

13. Black's, p. 1365.

14. Id. at p. 1365.

1. Give an example of a tort (civil wrong). _____

_____

_____

2. Give an example of a crime. _____

_____

_____

3. Why is it important for managers of park, recreation, and leisure service agencies to be aware of the doctrine of respondeat superior? _____

_____

_____

4. An ultra vires act is one that is outside the scope of duty or in excess of legal power or authority. Give an example of an ultra vires act. _____

_____

_____

5. List several ways in which administrators and supervisors can protect themselves from liability on the job. _____

_____

_____

6. T F A tort is a civil wrong independent of a contract that leads to personal injury or damage to property.

7. T F For all practical purposes, the doctrine of sovereign immunity can no longer be counted on as the first line of defense for governmental agencies.

8. T F The Federal Tort Claims Act was enacted in 1964.

9. T F Administrators and supervisors are not liable for the acts of their employees who may commit negligent acts unless they too were party to the act.

"Negligence in the popular sense is the lack of due diligence or care, but for legal purposes it is clear that there can be no negligence unless it is actionable negligence or a violation of the duty to use care."[1]

"Whether [negligence] exists depends, in each case, upon the particular circumstance ... on which the controversy is based."[2] "Negligence consists in the failure to exercise the care which an ordinarily prudent person would under the circumstances ... More particularly, actionable negligence [violation of a duty to use care] is the failure of one owing a duty to another to do what a reasonable and prudent person would ordinarily have done under the circumstances, or doing what such a person would not have done, which omission or commission is the proximate cause of injury to the other."[3]

ELEMENTS OF NEGLIGENCE

Prosser and Keeton's traditional formula defining the elements of negligence may be summarized as follows:[4]

1. A duty or obligation recognized by the law, requiring the person to conform to a certain standard of conduct for the protection of others against unreasonable risks.

2. A failure on the person's part to conform to the standard required: that is, a breach of the duty ...

3. A reasonably close causal connection between the conduct and the resulting injury ... [That is, the breach of duty was the "proximate cause" of the injury.]

4. Actual loss or damage resulting to the interests of another ...

All of these elements must be present and proved if the plaintiff is to recover damages.

THE LEGAL DUTY   Whether or not there is a legal duty in negligence cases is a question of law, it is something that is determined by the judge, not a jury. The court decides whether the level of conduct was sufficient to present unreasonable risk. According to Prosser and Keeton, unreasonable risk is conduct that falls below the standard established by law for the protection of others against unreasonable risk or harm.

"The requirement that a person exercise that care which the 'reasonable man' would exercise under 'similar circumstances' has persisted through the history of Anglo-American law," according to Dooley.[5] "This [also] was the view of Blackstone, who stated that the measure of the act was doing something or failing to do something which a reasonable man under the same or similar circumstances would have done or omitted."[6]

The reasonable man doctrine or standard of care compares the actions of a leader, teacher, coach, or supervisor with a reasonable man in the same or similar circumstances. The conduct of this hypothetical prudent and careful person will vary somewhat and likely combine both objective and subjective elements, including physical attributes, mental capacity, and special skills.

Regarding physical attributes, the reasonable person should possess those characteristics typical of his or her circumstances. If, by chance the person is mute, blind, deaf, or otherwise disabled, he or she must act as a reasonable person with the same infirmities. In other words, such persons are entitled to "live in the world" and to have allowances made for their disabilities.

When considering mental capacity, there is no allowance made for minor mental deficiencies, and defendants will be held to the test of reasonable conduct in the same manner as the prudent and careful person.

In regard to special skills, Prosser and Keeton are very clear: "Professional persons in general and those who undertake any work calling for special skill are required not only to exercise reasonable care in what they do, but also to possess a standard minimum of special knowledge and ability."[7] In other words park, recreation, and leisure service professionals will be held to a standard of care comparable to others employed in the field. Similarly, volunteers will be held accountable for special skills or knowledge that they claim to possess.

Rule of seven. The standard of care expected of children is not the same as for adults. Most courts recognize a minimum age below which a child cannot be held responsible. A number of states consider the age of seven as that minimum age; those six years and under are considered incapable of blame. Children between seven and thirteen are presumed to be incapable, and those from fourteen to majority age (age 21 and in some places age 18) are presumed to be capable but the opposite may be shown.

"These multiples of seven are derived originally from the Bible so say Prosser and Keeton, which is a poor reason for such arbitrary limits."[8] Some courts, however, reject such rules and indeed have held children well under age seven capable of some negligent conduct.

Doctrine of foreseeability. Like many aspects of the law, certain doctrines are very difficult to understand, much less explain. There is considerable confusion as to what is or is not foreseeable. Foreseeability is the ability to see or know in advance; a reasonable anticipation that harm or injury may result because of certain acts or omissions. "As a necessary element of proximate cause this means that the wrongdoer is not responsible for consequences which are merely possible, but is responsible only for consequence which is probable according to ordinary and usual experience."[9] Perhaps a more succinct way to put it would be to say the courts do not demand that you possess "mind-reading" skills, but they do expect one to anticipate risks to participants reasonably.

Finally, whether a legal duty exists is a question of law to be determined by the court (judge). It is the jury's responsibility to determine if the defendant conformed to a standard of care of reasonable prudence and foresight sufficient to protect the plaintiff against unreasonable risk.

THE BREACH OF DUTY (FAILURE TO CONFORM)   Once the duty of care has been established, the second element of negligence comes into play, that of failure to conform to the legal duty.

Betty van der Smissen says "negligent conduct may occur because of the manner in which a person acted (an act of commission) or because a person failed to act (an act of omission). Often used synonymously with act of commission and acts of omission are misfeasance and nonfeasance, respectively. This [van der Smissen says] is technically incorrect, since misfeasance may include both acts of commission and omission. The distinguishing factor is rather the nature of the person's participation in the enterprise (activity)."[10]

"There is a distinction between 'nonfeasance' and 'misfeasance' or 'malfeasance'; and this distinction is often of great importance in determining an agent's liability to third persons."[11]

Nonfeasance. "Nonperformance of some act which ought to be performed, omission to perform a required duty at all, or total neglect of duty."[12]

Misfeasance. "The improper performance of some act which a man may lawfully do."[13] This may include acts of commission as well as omission.

Malfeasance. "The doing of an act which person ought not to do at all. The commission of some act which is positively unlawful."[14]

"Res ipsa loquitur is rule of evidence whereby the negligence of the alleged wrongdoer may be inferred from the mere fact that the accident happened"; or "the thing speaks for itself."[15] Van der Smissen says that to apply the doctrine, two facts are necessary, although the presence of the two facts does not infer negligence: 1) the instrumentality must be under the exclusive control and management of the defendant and 2) the occurrence must be such that in the ordinary course of things it would not have happened if the defendant had used reasonable care.

The doctrine is further explained by Prosser and Keeton: "Where there is no direct evidence to show cause of injury and the circumstantial [detailed] evidence indicates that the negligence of the defendant is the most plausible explanation for the injury, the doctrine applies."[16]

PROXIMATE CAUSE   The third element in the formula defining negligence is "proximate cause." Whether or not the wrongful act was the proximate cause of the accident has been the subject of legal writers for generations. There is still much confusion and disagreement over the meaning of "proximate cause" or "legal cause." Negligence requires a causal relationship between the plaintiff and the defendant. Black's Law Dictionary expresses it this way: "An injury or damage is proximately caused by an act or failure to act whenever it appears from the evidence in the case that the act or omission played a substantial part in bringing about or actually causing the injury or damage; and that the injury or damage was either a direct result or a reasonable probable consequence of the act or omission."[17]

INJURY AND DAMAGES   The final and fourth element that must be present before negligence can be proved is injury. There must be actual loss or damage to the interests of another. There can be no negligence without injury to person or property.

<u>REMEMBER, UNLESS ALL FOUR ELEMENTS:</u>
<u>DUTY -- BREACH OF DUTY -- PROXIMATE CAUSE -- AND INJURY ARE PRESENT,</u>
<u>NEGLIGENCE CANNOT BE FOUND.</u>

The word "damage" refers to "loss, injury, or deterioration caused by the negligence, design, or accident of one person to another in respect of the latter's person or property."[18] However, the word "damages" refers to compensation in the form of money for a loss or damage. "Damages may be compensatory or punitive according to whether they are awarded as the measure of actual loss suffered or as punishment for outrageous conduct and to deter future transgressions."[19]

"<u>Compensatory damages</u> are those awarded to a person as compensation, indemnity, or restitution for harm sustained by him."[20]

<u>Punitive or exemplary damages</u> "may be awarded against [a] person to punish him for outrageous conduct."[21]

<u>Consequential damages</u> are "those losses or injuries which are a result of an act but are not direct and immediate."[22]

There are also many other forms of damages, such as continual, criminal, direct, excessive, expectance, fee, land, and others that would be well to add to your vocabulary.

DEGREE OF NEGLIGENCE

Some authorities suggest that there is no "degree" of care in negligence as a matter of law; there are only different amounts of care as a matter of the fact.[23] However, since the following terms are frequently used and still recognized in some jurisdictions, a brief explanation of the more commonly used degrees of negligence is in order.

<u>Ordinary negligence</u> is defined as "the failure to exercise such care as the great mass of mankind ordinarily exercises under the same or similar circumstances...."[24]

<u>Gross negligence</u> is defined as "very great negligence or as the want of even slight care...."[25]

<u>Willful, wanton, or reckless negligence</u> is where "the conduct complained of is so 'gross' as to have something of a criminal character, or be deemed equivalent to an evil intent, wantonness, or recklessness, or indicative of malice."[26]

REMEMBER, not all jurisdictions recognize degrees of negligence, so look to your legal counsel for an interpretation in your jurisdiction.

Defenses in negligence cases are given as reasons in law or fact either to diminish or defeat the plaintiff's charges. The major defenses are:
- contributory negligence
- comparative negligence
- assumption of risk
- act of God
- governmental immunity
- waivers, releases, agreements to participate

CONTRIBUTORY NEGLIGENCE   At one time this was one of the main defenses in negligence cases. If it could be established that the plaintiff was negligent, even to the slightest degree, there could be no recovery of damages.

Most everyone agreed that this extremely harsh all-or-nothing common law rule was blatantly unfair. Following the lead of the federal statutes, states began enacting comparative negligence statutes. Mississippi was the first state to enact a comparative negligence statute in 1910. Today, 45 states, Puerto Rico, and the Virgin Islands have adopted some form of comparative negligence scheme. (See Figure 2 for a complete listing.)

Essentially then, contributory negligence can be used as a defense in only five states, and it is probably only a matter of time until those five states adopt some form of comparative negligence.

COMPARATIVE NEGLIGENCE   Unlike the old common law contributory negligence rule where the plaintiff could not recover if he or she was slightly at fault, the comparative negligence laws allow for damages even if the plaintiff's fault is rather substantial.   The four main classifications of comparative negligence are:

1. Pure comparative negligence. This form abolishes the contributory negligence exclusion completely unless the plaintiff is 100 per cent negligent; the plaintiff's total damages are reduced in proportion to the amount of negligence attributable to him or her.

2. 50 per cent rule. The plaintiff is barred from recovery if his or her negligence is greater than that of the defendant.

3. 49 per cent rule. Recovery is barred unless the plaintiff's negligence is less than that of the defendant.

4. Slight-gross rule. Recovery is barred unless the plaintiff's negligence was slight and the defendant's was gross by comparison.[27]

Figure 1 gives examples of pure comparative negligence, the 50% Rule and the 49% Rule.[28]

```
┌─────────────────────────────────────────────────────────────────────────────┐
│                    FIGURE 1.  COMPARATIVE NEGLIGENCE EXAMPLES                  │
├──────────────────────────────────────────┬────────────────────────────────────┤
│ Example 1:  Pure Comparative Negligence   │ Example 4:  The 49% Rule           │
```

FIGURE 1. COMPARATIVE NEGLIGENCE EXAMPLES

Example 1: Pure Comparative Negligence		Example 4: The 49% Rule	
Plaintiff's share of the negligence:	20%	Plaintiff;s share of negligence:	35%
Defendant's share of the negligence:	80%	Defendant's share of negligence:	65%
Plaintiff's damages:	$10,000	Plaintiff's damages:	$20,000
Share of damage attributable to		Plaintiff's recoverable damages:	
plaintiff's negligence:		$20,000 x 0.65 =	$13,000.
$10,000 x 0.20 =	$ 2,000		
Plaintiff's judgment against defendant:			
$10,000 - 2,000 =	$ 8,000		

Example 2: The 50% Rule		Example 5: The 49% Rule	
Plaintiff's share of negligence:	35%	Plaintiff's share of negligence:	50%
Defendant's share of negligence:	65%	Defendant's share of negligence:	50%
Plaintiff's damages:	$20,000	Plaintiff's damages:	$10,000
Plaintiff's recoverable damages:		Plaintiff's recoverable damages: Barred	
$20,000 x 0.65 =	$13,000	Under the 49% Rule, an equally neg-	
Under the 50% Rule, an equally negligent		ligent plaintiff is barred from recovery.	
plaintiff is permitted to recover.			

Example 3: The 50% Rule		Examples taken from Comparative Negligence,
Plaintiff's share of negligence:	50%	V. 1, Chapter 2., pp. 2 - 5, 2 - 30.
Defendant's share of negligence:	50%	(New York: Matthew Bender, May 1986).
Plaintiff's damages:	$20,000	
Plaintiff's recoverable damages:		
$20,000 x 0.50 =	$10,000	

ASSUMPTION OF RISK   This is the second primary defence in negligence cases, and it means that persons may not recover for injuries received when they voluntarily expose themselves to a known and appreciated danger. Requirements are that:

1. "The plaintiff has knowledge of facts constituting a dangerous condition,
2. he knows the condition is dangerous,
3. he appreciates the nature or extent of the danger, and
4. he voluntarily exposes himself to the danger."[29] (See section on releases/waivers.)

It is important for park, recreation, and leisure service personnel to understand that participants cannot assume risk for something of which they are ignorant,where they do not comprehend the risk in relationship to their physical and mental capabilities, nor appreciate the magnitude of possible injury.

Participants only assume the risk for aspects inherent in the activity. They may properly assume that it is the duty of the sponsoring agency to provide appropriate and safe facilities, equipment, instruction, and supervision.

ACT OF GOD   "No liability attaches when the proximate cause is an Act of God, a condition caused by the natural elements."[30]

GOVERNMENTAL IMMUNITY   In the federal government and in most states, the doctrine has been abolished either by the courts or state general assemblies.

STATUTE OF LIMITATIONS   These are statutes enacted to limit the time in which actions may be brought for certain claims. Statutes of limitations vary by state. Careful analysis of these statutes in your state would be a prudent exercise.

FIGURE 2.0.
SUMMARY OF STATES ADOPTING COMPARATIVE NEGLIGENCE SCHEMES.*

Forty-five states, Puerto Rico, and the Virgin Islands have adopted comparative negligence plans.

States With Pure Comparative Negligence

Arizona	By Legislative Enactment
Louisiana	" "
Mississippi	" "
New York	" "
Rhode Island	" "
Washington	" "
Puerto Rico	" "

Alaska	By Judicial Adoption
California	" "
Florida	" "
Illinois	" "
Iowa	" "
Kentucky	" "
Michigan	" "
Missouri	" "
New Mexico	" "

States With 50% Rule

Connecticut
Delaware
Hawaii
Indiana
Massachusetts
Minnesota
Montana
Nevada
New Hampshire
New Jersey
Ohio
Oklahoma
Oregon
Pennsylvania
Texas
Vermont
Wisconsin
Virgin Islands

States With 49% Rule
Arkansas
Colorado
Georgia
Idaho
Kansas
Maine
North Dakota
Utah
West Virginia
Wyoming

States With Slight-Gross Rule
Nebraska
South Dakota
Tennessee

States Without Comparative
    Negligence Principles
Alabama
Maryland
North Carolina
South Carolina
Virginia

*Source: Comparative Negligence Law and Practice, Vol. 1, Chapters 1 - 9.

14

WAIVERS, RELEASES, AND AGREEMENTS TO PARTICIPATE   While all the defenses up to now have had their bases in tort law, waivers and releases are considered exculpatory clauses designed to absolve, exonerate, acquit, or indemnify (hold harmless) the sponsoring agencies from loss. They are based in contract law and therefore do not pertain to minors.

On the other hand, agreements to participate stay with two legal concepts discussed earlier: the assumption of risk and contributory negligence. Agreements to participate are not contracts, and minors may sign.

Waivers and Releases. Since minors are unable to contract, the use of waivers and releases is considered improper. There is awareness and psychological value attached to having minors sign waivers and/or releases but little else. "For an exculpatory [hold harmless] clause to be upheld in court, van der Smissen says it must meet the criteria for a valid contract. The critical principles to be met include:"

  a. Persons must be of majority age; minors may ratify upon reaching majority [may vary by state];

  b. it must not be against public policy, it cannot be a nondelegable duty to protect and there usually must be an alternative for the participant;

  c. it must be voluntarily signed; it cannot be an "adhesion" contract, in which the participant really has not choice; and

  d. it must be very explicit, using clear language that states release or indemnification for negligence of defendant; awareness and understanding are not required if they are obvious and clear in written form ....[31]

Contracts have been held valid, primarily for adventure sports such as whitewater rafting, sky diving, or parachuting. While contracts meeting the criteria are now being upheld, one should not depend upon such exculpatory clauses to avoid liability. Also, there is some question as to the ethics of such clauses. If indeed a defendant was negligent and caused injury, should not the injured plaintiff receive redress?

Agreement to participate. Minors cannot sign away their right to sue. Parents can only sign away their right to sue on the child's behalf but cannot sign away the child's right to sue.

Agreements to participate were explained by van der Smissen in the *National Safety Network Newsletter.* [32]

> Since minors can't waive negligence, an agreement to participate can be used since this applies to any age. The agreement to participate goes to two legal concepts, the assumption of risk and contributory negligence. The agreement to participate is not a contract, but a signed statement that the participant understands the dangers inherent in the activity or program, that they appreciate the consequences of the risks involved, including the possibility of injury and death that could result from participation.

There are criteria for designing an effective agreement to participate or assumption of risk.

  1. It must be explicitly worded.

  2. If there are rules that must be followed, they should be listed in the agreement or on the reverse side of the paper. Wording should be included that the participant has received the rules if they are not included, has read and understands them, and will abide by them.

3. The possible dangers inherent in the activities must be spelled out in detail along with the consequences of possible accidents so the participant can appreciate the risks and their possible consequences. The participant must sign a statement expressly assuming the risks of participation.

For the assumption of risk defense to hold in court, the risks of an activity must be described in detail. For instance, in a rock climbing program it must be said that the risks include the possibility of falling from a cliff and being bodily injured including death, or the possibility of being hit by falling rocks dislodged by others or by the forces of nature that could result in severe injury or death. In a rafting or canoeing program the language should describe the dangers of falling from or being thrown from a raft and the possibility of being in cold water for a long time, hitting rocks or other obstructions in the water, being pinned against a rock, including the possibility of suffering hypothermia or drowning. Releases are held without such detailed descriptions, but for an agreement to participate to be useful the description must be vivid and understandable to the individual participant.

One seeming paradox is that it is less risky, from the legal viewpoint for an organization to operate advanced skills activities than to operate activities for beginners. Your organization will be held to a stricter protective care and supervisory role with beginners than with advanced participants who, in theory at least, understand the nature of the dangers because they are experienced and therefore sign an agreement to participate with greater knowledge.

For maximum benefit you should consider using releases and waivers for adult participants and releases signed by parents of minors attached to an agreement to participate signed by the minor.

CASE STUDIES

The following cases are included to give the reader an opportunity to see how certain elements such as due care, proximate cause, foreseeability, and so forth are being treated by the judicial system.

YOU SHOULD NOT TRANSLATE THE CASES OR DECISIONS DIRECTLY TO YOUR PARTICULAR AREA SINCE VARIOUS COURTS AND STATES MAY PLACE THEIR OWN INTERPRETATION ON THE FACTS OF THE CASE. USE THE IDEAS PRESENTED IN THESE CASES AS A BASIS OF DISCUSSION WITH YOUR STAFF AND LEGAL COUNSEL.

SPECTATOR INJURED AT SOFTBALL GAME

Swagger v. City of Crystal
379 N.W. 2d. 183 (Minn. App. 1985)
Court of Appeals of Minnesota
December 24, 1985

This case reflects on a rather common occurrence. "The plaintiff was attending a softball game on July 25, 1981, at Welcome Park Field No. 3, which is owned and operated by defendant, City of Crystal, Minnesota."

The softball game was part of the 1981 "Crystal Frolics," sponsored by Crystal's Parks and Recreation Department. Darlene Swagger had never played softball; however, she had watched little league baseball and softball games her husband had played.

One set of bleachers was behind the backstop and another set between home plate and first base. The seating capacity of the bleachers was 50 - 70 persons. The crowd numbered between 600 and 1,000 people. The Swaggers found the bleachers full. They found a spot to watch the game about six feet past first base towards the outfield and about 30 feet from the first base line.

During the game, Darlene Swagger was injured when struck in the face by a wildly thrown softball. As a result of this injury she suffered severe and permanent injuries to her nose and right eye.

The defendant Swagger argued that "the owner of the ball park had a duty to protect spectators." However, the court stated that "this argument is not supported by Minnesota law."

The trial court directed a verdict based on primary assumption of risk. In Minnesota this means that "the defendant owed no duty of care toward the plaintiff and therefore could not be guilty of negligence with respect to him."

[The court stated] that the management cannot be held negligent when it provides a choice between a screened in and an open seat, the screen being sufficient in extent and substance. The court also held that the management need not provide screened seats for all who want them: In our opinion they exercise the required care if they provide screening for the most dangerous part of the grandstand and for those who may be reasonably anticipated to desire protected seats, and that they need not provide seats for an unusual crowd ...

The court added:

In our opinion no adult of reasonable intelligence, even with the limited experience of the plaintiff, could fail to realize that he would be injured if he were struck by a thrown or batted ball such as is used in league games of the character which he was observing, nor could he fail to realize that foul balls were likely to be directed toward where he was sitting. No one of ordinary intelligence could see many innings of the ordinary league game without coming to a full realization that batters cannot and do not control the direction of the ball***

The appeals court agreed with the trial court in this case saying, "There was not duty to the appellants [Swagger] to do other than provide some protected seating."

WOMEN ASSAULTED IN UNATTENDED LOCKER ROOM

482 N.Y.S. 2D 613 (A.D. 4 Dept. 1984)
Supreme Court, Appellate Division, Fourth Department
November 7, 1984

This case has elements of several principles discussed throughout the manual, namely duty owed, due care, proximate cause, injury, landowner, and foreseeability.

Plaintiff, Helen Montag was assaulted in an unattended women's locker room in the YMCA of

Oneida County, New York. The attack was by an unidentified male assailant on premises maintained by the defendant YMCA.

In this rather unusual case, the trial court granted a motion to dismiss the case while the jury was still deliberating. "[T]he court granted [the] defendant's motion to dismiss the complaint, finding as a matter of law that [the] plaintiff had failed to establish foreseeability or the existence of a duty owed by the defendant."

The jury was however permitted to continue its deliberations and was allowed to enter its findings.

> "The jury awarded [the] plaintiff $50,000 based on its unanimous findings that (1) the plaintiff had been assaulted and injured; (2) defendant was negligent in providing or maintaining security in the women's section of its premises; (3) defendant's negligence was the proximate cause of plaintiff's injuries; and (4) plaintiff was entitled to $6,245 in medical expenses and lost wages and $43,755 for pain and suffering."

In light of the jury findings, the plaintiff appealed to the appellate court and the court agreed there was sufficient evidence from which the jury could have found the defendant (YMCA) negligent.

The evidence indicated that the defendant YMCA was aware of the need for security, and had, in effect, instituted security measures. "There was a security desk staffed by a YMCA employee directly outside the entrance to the locker room, but at the time of the assault, the employee was absent from her post." Thus the defendant's negligence was the proximate cause of the plaintiff's injuries.

"The duty owed by the YMCA to the plaintiff is that of a landowner who must maintain his property in a reasonable safe condition ...."

"Under such a standard, a landlord has a duty to maintain minimal security measures, related to a specific building itself, in the face of foreseeable criminal intrusion upon tenants."

The appellate court agreed that the defendant (YMCA) was negligent in that it failed to exercise due care required under the circumstances. The appellate court said that the trial court erred in dismissing the complaint and reinstated the jury's verdict.

UNGUARDED BEACH DROWNING AT NATIONAL LAKESHORE

Clem v. United States
601 F. Supp. 835 (1985)
United States District Court, N.D. Indiana
January 29, 1985

In this drowning case Mary Clem, the plaintiff, brought suit against the United States to recover damages for the wrongful death of her husband, Cary Lee Clem. The Indiana Dunes National Lakeshore Park operated by the National Park Service (NPS) was the location of the drowning.

The defendant (United States) was granted a motion to dismiss on the following grounds:

(1) Indiana recreational use statute barred any recovery by widow.
(2) Even assuming National Park Service was negligent in some way, service did not breach any duty owed to licensee.

(3) Decedent was guilty of contributory negligence.

(4) Doctrine of incurred risk prevented widow from recovering damages.

A closer review of these factors indicates why the court ruled the way it did. In part, the Indiana Recreational Use Statute (I.C. 14-2-6-3) provides:

> Any person who goes upon ... the premises ... lands, caves, waters ... of another with or without permission to hunt, fish, swim, trap, camp, hike, sightsee, or for any other purpose, without the payment of monetary consideration ... is not thereby entitled to any assurance that the premises are safe for such purpose. The owner of such premises does not assume responsibility for, nor incur any liability for, any injury to person or property caused by an act or failure to act of other persons using such premises.
>
> The provision of this section shall not be construed as affecting the existing case law of Indiana of liability of owners or possessors of premises with respect to business invitees in commercial establishments nor to invited guests, nor shall this section be construed as to affect the attractive nuisance doctrine. Nothing in this section shall excuse the owner or occupant of premises from liability for injury to persons or property caused by the malicious or illegal acts of the owner or occupant.

The court found that the Clems "were engaged in an activity explicitly covered by the statute." The only issue remaining was whether any of the exceptions stated in the statute such as admission fees, attractive nuisance, and malicious misconduct were applicable.

> The Clems paid no admission fee nor was one paid on their behalf in gaining access to the Park or to its various facilities. Thus, no economic benefit was derived by the federal government so as to trigger operation of the statute's consideration exception. Further, there is no issue involving an attractive nuisance nor allegations by the plaintiff that the alleged injury was caused by any malicious or illegal acts of the federal government.

Since none of the above exceptions applied, the Clems based their case in part on the invited guest exception.

> The evidence in the case presently before the court clearly indicates that the Clems were licensees, not invitees. The Clems entered the Park and used the facilities there for their own entertainment. They were not on the Park's premises to transact business, do some act to benefit the NPS, nor do some act that was a mutual benefit to them and the NPS. Although the plaintiff argues that an implied invitation arose due to the acts and conduct of the NPS, including the facts that the Park was maintained for the use of the public, the Park maintained a Visitors Center, employed rangers, posted various directional signs, and maintained parking lots and toilet facilities, these facts do not constitute an "implied invitation" within the meaning of the invitee. Rather, the Clems' presence on the premises of the Park, if by "implied invitation" was more in the nature of a social guest which under Indiana law has only the rights of a licensee, not an invitee. Accordingly, the Clems had the status of licensee under Indiana law.

The court rules that the "invited guest" exception claimed by the Clems pertains only to the invitee category under Indiana law. The court therefore refused to include the Clems as "invited guests" within the licensee category and barred recovery by the plaintiff in this area.

Since the Clems entered as licensees, "they took the land as they found it and cannot hold the owner thereof liable for any defects in the condition of the land." Regarding the breach of duty claim, the duty owed, in this case, is to restrain from wilfully or wantonly injuring the plaintiff or acting in a way that would increase the licensee's peril.

At the time of the accident, contributory negligence was a complete defense in Indiana. That is, if the plaintiff's actions "were unreasonable under the circumstances so as to constitute lack of ordinary care, and contributed to his death by any degree, the plaintiff is barred from recovery."

> Bases on this evidence, the court finds that Mr. Clem did not exercise reasonable care for a person of like age, intelligence, and experience under similar circumstances and thus was contributorily negligent. Although Mr. Clem may not have known of the specific danger of undertow on July 28, 1982, a person of like age, intelligence, and experience, or lack thereof with respect to large bodies of water, exercising reasonable care, would not have gone swimming at Mt. Baldy, an unguarded area.

Note: Indiana has adopted a comparative negligence statute (I.C. 34-4-33-1 et seq.) effective January 1, 1985.

Finally, in this case the court also ruled that the doctrine of incurred risk did apply. This means that an individual "incurs all the ordinary and usual risks of an act upon which [he] the actor voluntarily enters, so long as those risks are known and understood by the actor."

> The Clems made a conscious, deliberate, and voluntary decision to go swimming in Lake Michigan at Mt. Baldy Beach, an unguarded beach. They had been warned that the waters of Lake Michigan could be treacherous and had viewed a film containing a safety message about swimming in the lake. They had read and discussed a sign that clearly stated that no lifeguards were on duty and thus were aware that no professional help was provided in the event that they encountered trouble. Under Indiana law, one of the recognized risks of swimming, particularly in a large body of unfamiliar water of unknown propensities, is drowning. Added to this knowledge on the part of the Clems is the additional knowledge they had, and thus the acceptance of the risk that the waters could be treacherous, even though they may not have known every aspect that made them so as well as the risk inherent in swimming at an unguarded beach. Accordingly, the doctrine of incurred risk applies and prevents recovery by plaintiff in this action.

The court granted the defendant's motion for dismissal but with this added admonition: "The human heart strings pull in one direction and the law compels a contrary conclusion." The court also suggested that "sympathy cannot be the basis of a decision."

NOTES CHAPTER II

1. 57 Am. Jur. 2d, Municipal, School, and State Tort Liability, Sec. 1, p. 333 (1971).

2. Id. at Sec. 1, p. 334.

3. Id. at Sec.1, pp. 334-335.

4. W. Prosser and W. Keeton, The Law of Torts, 5th ed. (St. Paul: West Publishing Co., 1984) pp. 164-165.

5. Dooley Mod. Tort Law, Sec. 3.06, p. 24 (1982).

6. Id. at pp. 24-25.

7. Prosser and Keeton, p. 185.

8. Id. at p. 180.

9. Black's Law Dictionary (5th ed. 1979), p. 584.

10. Betty van der Smissen, Legal Liability of Cities and Schools for Injuries in Recreation and Parks (Cincinnati: W.H. Anderson Co., 1968) pp. 78-79.

11. Black's, p. 950.

12. Id. at p. 950.

13. Id. at p. 902.

14. Id. at p. 862.

15. Id. at p. 1173.

16. Prosser and Keeton, p. 257.

17. Black's, p. 1103.

18. Id. at p. 351.

19. Id. at p. 352.

20. Id. at p. 352.

21. Id. at p. 352.

22. Id. at p. 352.

23. Id. at p. 931.

24. 57 Am. Jur. 2d, Sec. 98, p. 447.

25. Id. at p. 447.

26. Id. at p. 448.

27. Comparative Negligence, Vol. 1., Chapter 2.

28. Id. at pp. 2-5, 2-20.

29. Black's, p. 113.

30. van der Smissen, p. 92.

31. Address by Betty van der Smissen, 40th Annual Great Lakes Park Training Institute (Feb. 24, 1986). Published in 40th Annual Proceedings of the Great Lakes Park Training Institute, Indiana University, Bloomington, IN (1986).

32. National Safety Network Newsletter, Vol. 1, No. 4, (March, 1985).

1. In order for a plaintiff (complaining party) to recover damages, all four elements of negligence must be present. The first element is the duty or obligation that requires a person to conform to a certain standard. This is determined by the court. The other three essentials of negligence are:

   _____

   _____

   _____

2. Some states consider children under seven years of age incapable of blame. How does your state treat young defendants under seven years? Those between seven and fourteen years? And those from fifteen years to the age of majority? (Consult with legal counsel.)

3. Distinguish between the following:
   Nonfeasance_____

   (Give an example.) _____

   Misfeasance _____

   (Give an example.) _____

   Malfeasance_____

   (Give an example.) _____

4. According to Figure 2, my state of _____ falls into the category of comparative negligence.

5. The statute of limitations - - that is, the time limit on when claims may be filed varies by state. The limitations in my state are _____
   _____ . (Consult with legal counsel.)

6. Waivers and releases are satisfactory for use by adults providing certain criteria are met. Identify those criteria. _____

   _____

7. A breach of duty can be caused by acts of omission or commission. Give an example of each.

   _____

   _____

8. What is meant by proximate or legal cause in relationship to negligence? _____

   _____

   _____

9. Distinguish between
   a. Compensatory damages: _____

   b. Punitive or exemplary damages: _____

   c. Consequential damages: _____

10. What comparative negligence scheme does your state provide
   a. Pure comparative negligence
   b. 50 per cent rule
   c. 49 per cent rule
   d. Slight-gross rule
   e. My state is without comparative negligence principles.

11. What is an exculpatory clause? Can minors sign them? _____

_____

_____

12. Since an "agreement to participate" is not a contract and therefore permissible for minors to sign, what criteria are necessary for an effective agreement? _____

_____

13. T F   It is permissible for minors to sign waivers and releases because they are exculpatory clauses.

14. T F   Under the 50 per cent rule of comparative negligence, the plaintiff cannot recover damages if his negligence is more than the defendant's.

15. T F   The 50 per cent rule of comparative negligence is distinguished from the 49 per cent rule by virtue of the fact that the 50 per cent rule permits a negligent plaintiff to recover from an equally negligent defendant. The 49 per cent rule bars recovery unless the plaintiff's negligence is less than that of the defendant.

16. T F   The 49 per cent rule permits a plaintiff to recover provided his or her share of the negligence is less than that of the defendant.

CHAPTER III. STANDARD OF CARE OWED BY OWNERS, OPERATORS, AND MANAGERS

This chapter addresses the standard of care that owners, operators, and managers of park, recreation, and leisure services facilities owe to their users. The determination of a visitor's status is a critical element in deciding what standard of care must be provided.

In general, persons who visit park, recreation, and leisure facilities, whether public or private, are classified as invitees, licensees or trespassers. The duty owed to each can and does vary. Basically, the invitee receives the most protection under the law, the licensee some protection, and the trespasser the least protection. The information that follows is intended to acquaint you with this important area of tort liability. It will re-introduce familiar terms that can be complicated and confusing at times. Use this section to open a dialogue with your legal counsel to determine how the terms are treated and interpreted in your area.

INVITEES

An invitee, one who is at a place at the invitation of another, is described in the Restatement (Second) of tort §332.

(1)   An invitee is either a public invitee or a business visitor.

(2)   A public invitee is a person who is invited to enter or remain on land as a member of the public for a purpose for which the land is held open to the public.

(3)   A business visitor is a person who is invited to enter or remain on land for a purpose directly or indirectly connected with business dealing with the possessor of the land.

In the case of invitees, the owner, operators, and managers have a duty to assure that reasonable care has been used to prepare the premises and make them safe for the visitors. This includes protection from injury related to the condition of the land, facilities, or equipment or by injury from third parties. In the case of invitees the owner, operator, or manager must inspect the premises, remove or warn of potential hazards, and as a general rule exercise reasonable care to protect users.

A person's status may change due to time and location. For example, one is an invitee to a public park that is open from sunup to sundown. However, after sundown, if the park is officially closed, the invitee status may change to that of trespasser, thereby altering the duty owed by the owner, operator, or manager.

LICENSEES

A licensee is described in Restatement (Second) of tort §330.

A licensee is a person who is privileged to enter or remain on land only by virtue of the possessor's [owner's, manager's] consent.

"A[n] owner owes to a licensee no duty as to the condition of the premises (unless imposed by statute) save that he should not knowingly let him run upon a hidden peril or willfully cause him harm; while to one invited he is under the obligation to maintain the premises in a reasonably safe and secure condition."[1]

There is a distinction made between a "bare" licensee that is one whose presence is merely tolerated, and a licensee by invitation or a "social guest." Although a social guest may be invited and even urged to come, he is not an "invitee" within the legal meaning of that term according to Restatement (Second) of tort §330. The social guest is no more than a licensee and is expected to take the premises as the owner himself uses them.

TRESPASSERS

A trespasser is "one who intentionally and without consent or privilege enters another's property."[2]

Owners, operators, and managers owe adult trespassers a duty of care similar to that of a licensee. They have no duty to make their property or facilities reasonably safe or to warn of dangerous conditions. They only have a duty to avoid injury by intentional, reckless, and wanton misconduct.

ATTRACTIVE NUISANCES In the case of trespassing children, the Attractive Nuisance doctrine comes into play. Essentially, owners who have created artificial or man-made conditions where they have reason to believe that children may trespass, or where the land possesses something that may be expected to attract children, are under duty to provide such care as a reasonably prudent person would take to prevent injury. These provisions do not apply to natural conditions, only artificial conditions.

RECREATIONAL USE STATUTE In recent years almost all states (see page 3 for a more detailed discussion) have enacted recreational use statutes that provide some protection to public and private land owners who allow their property to be used for public recreation purposes. A careful analysis of your state's recreation use statutes would be a prudent exercise.

CASE STUDIES

The following cases describe some of the subtleties that bear on the interpretation of a visitor's status. A clear understanding of this phenomenon will be helpful in determining the standard of care required of owners, operators, and managers of park, recreation, and leisure services.

The following case[3] illustrates how the school board owed no duty to the plaintiff, a bare licensee, who was six years old and who was injured when she touched exposed electrical wires at [the] base of [an] electrical light pole located in a high school parking lot, where board had no actual knowledge that wires were exposed or knowledge that the plaintiff and her companions were in the parking lot after school hours to watch the plaintiff's brother and his friends ride a go-cart.

THE UNDISPUTED FACTS

Fitzgerald v. Montgomery County Board of Education
25 MD. APP. 709, 1975
Court of Special Appeals of Maryland

Allyn M. Fitzgerald was 6 years of age. On 15 June 1972, her father took her, her mother, her brother, age 15 years, and Stubbings, a friend of the brother, also 15 years of age, to the parking lot of Margruder High School, owned and maintained by appelle. They arrived between 6:15 and 6:30, long after school hours. The purpose of the trip was to enable the brother and his friend to ride a go-cart on the lot. There was an electric light pole on the lot, mounted on a concrete pillar about two and a half feet high. Allyn stood on this pillar. The metal cover had been removed from an opening in the pole, and protruding therefrom were three wires carrying 227 volts of electrical current. Allyn's legs came in contact with these live wires and she received an electrical shock. Her father found her on the ground unconscious and applied mouth-to-mouth resuscitation until she regained consciousness. Her legs were burned and she was taken to the hospital. No warning had been given by appellee to appellants with respect to the exposed wires. Although Stubbings stated in his deposition he observed the exposed wires two weeks before when he was riding a go-cart on the lot, appellee had no actual knowledge that they were exposed. Nor did appellee know that appellants were on the parking lot. It had not given them or those who accompanied them permission to use the lot for go-cart riding. None of those involved attended the school nor were they engaged in school activities when the accident occurred.

The court granted a summary judgment (immediate, without a jury) in favor of the school board, and the plaintiffs appealed. The summary judgment was upheld by the Court of Special Appeals.

The standard of care in this jurisdiction owed by an owner of real property to a bare licensee or trespasser is essentially what is known as the Massachusetts rule, under which the owner's sole duty is to abstain from intentional injury. In this case, the defendant board of education owed no duty to the plaintiff who was considered a bare licensee. The board had no knowledge that wires were exposed or knowledge that the plaintiff and her companions were in the parking lot after school hours. The board had not given permission for the plaintiff and her companions to use the parking lot for go-cart riding.

Additional cases that follow will highlight various interpretations relating to invitees, licensees, and trespassers.

GOLF CART ACCIDENT

United States v. Marshall
391 F. 2d 880, 883, citing 330 - 32
Court of Appeals 1st Circuit, 1968[4]

The plaintiff, who was playing golf on a course owned by the defendant at the invitation of another, was injured when trying to protect herself and a male companion from a sudden rainstorm. She drove a golf cart they were using off the fairway, into high grass, and, to her suprise, into a ravine. There the cart overturned, injuring her. The plaintiff claimed that the defendant, as a landowner, was negligent in failing to meet the standard of care due her as a social guest - invitee under Puerto Rican law which controlled the case, or, alternatively, the care due her as a licensee. After finding that Puerto Rican law accepted the common law rule that social guests are not invitees but licensees, the court held that the defendant had no reason to believe anyone would drive a cart into such a remote part of the course, it had not breached its duty to the licensee-plaintiff to warn her of a condition it should have recognized would pose an unreasonable risk of harm to her.

HOT EMBERS, LEASED LAND

Chandler v. Mass
415 F. 2d 560, 568
cert.denied 397 U.S. 996, 25 L. Ed. 2d 404
90 S. Ct. 1137, 1970
Court of Appeals 6th Circuit, 1969[5]

This was an action for injuries sustained by a four-year-old boy when he stepped on ashes covering hot embers in a pasture leased by a saddle club from defendants. In affirming the lower courts directed verdict for defendants, the court held that the landlord's attempt to extinguish a smouldering fire on the leased pasture by spreading the burning embers did not constitute setting a "trap," and that no duty to plaintiff was breached.

NOTES CHAPTER III

1. Black's Law Dictionary, Revised Fourth Edition, p. 960.

2. Black's Law Dictionary, Fifth Edition, p. 1348.

3. Fitzgerald v. Montgomery County Bd. of Ed., 25 Md. App. 709, 336 A. 2d, pp.795-797.

4. American Law Institute, Restatement of the Law Second, Torts 2d. App. Vol. Sec. 310-402 (1964-1975), p. 11.

5. Id. at p. 20.

1. Distinguish between:

    A. An invitee _____

    (Give an example.) _____

    B. A licensee _____

    (Give an example.) _____

    C. A trespasser _____

    (Give an example.) _____

2. The terms invitee, licensee, and trespasser are interpreted differently in various parts of the country. Why? _____

    _____

    _____

    _____

3. Under the law, child and adult trespassers are treated differently. How? _____

    _____

    _____

    _____

4. T   F   An invited "social guest" is treated as a licensee in the eyes of the law.

WHY HAVE A PLAN?

With a risk management plan, you will be taking a pro-active approach to managing risk. You will project an attitude that says, "We have an obligation to permit users to have quality leisure experiences in safe surroundings."

It is a philosophy that protects against undue risk.

It is a planned program that minimizes risk through professionally desirable practices and tells everyone:

YES, WE ARE KNOWLEDGEABLE PROFESSIONALS, WE ARE CONCERNED FOR YOUR SAFETY, AND WE WILL DO WHAT IS NECESSARY TO PROVIDE A SAFE ENVIRONMENT FOR YOUR LEISURE ACTIVITIES.

A secondary benefit or reason for taking one's professional responsibility seriously is that in the event of legal action, a solid pro-active program shows intent. A program of managing risk serves as a deterrent to being sued and, if sued, as evidence of intent to act responsibly.

WHO IS RESPONSIBLE ?

Many of the accidents that occur daily can be prevented. In fact, many are being prevented or severely reduced by those managerial teams who develop and execute a program of risk management focusing on reasonable care.

Sounds simple doesn't it?

As responsible professionals we must develop a plan, initiate it, and act responsibly.

The challenge comes in understanding the procedure, the reasons why we do something, and who is responsible. Consider the following questions as the risk management plan begins to unfold.

- Who authorizes it?
- Who develops it?
- Who carries it out?
- What is in the plan?

Before addressing the "what," let's describe the "who." Who is responsible? Everyone's responsibility is no one's responsibility. This old adage is not applicable with a risk management plan.

For a plan to be effective, it is everyone's responsibility. However, the constant effort of a key coordinator is needed to assist, guide, train, motivate, and consult with staff throughout the system to accomplish the agency goals.

Figure 3 illustrates everyone's responsibility. Regardless of agency size, any risk management plan should have the blessing and authority of the governing body : be it a park and recreation board or commission, an agency board, a school board, or a private corporation governing body. The establishment of a policy by the governing or corporate structure legitimizes their position and tells the staff and users of its facilities and programs that they believe in the concept. They are willing to allow staff to devote the necessary resources to develop and carry out such a plan. By authorizing and ultimately approving the plan, the corporate structure is making its statement for responsibility in managing risk.

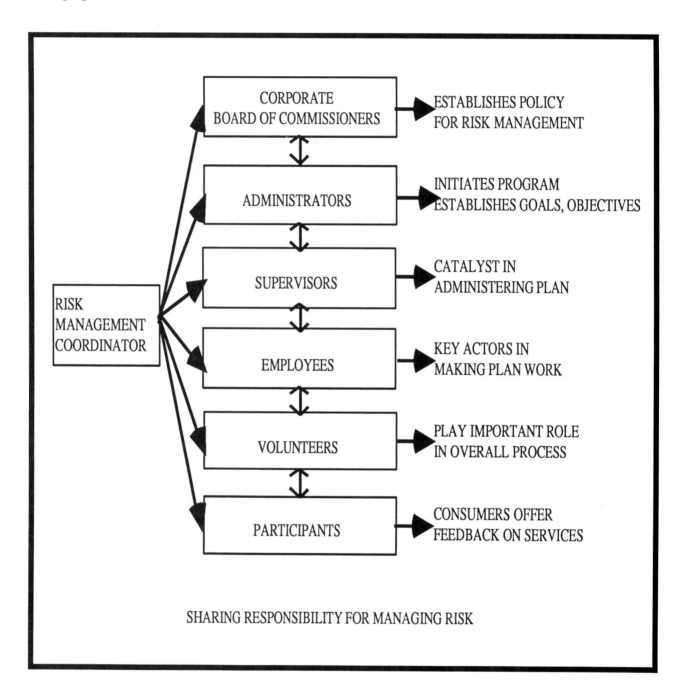

SHARING RESPONSIBILITY FOR MANAGING RISK

The *administrator's* role is to carry out the wishes of the board or governing authority and determine the best method to develop and monitor a risk management plan. The size of the department or agency will be a determining factor. In smaller units, the administrator may be responsible. In larger units a risk management officer may be assigned on a full-time basis. In most departments, however, the duty will be coupled with other administrative functions. In larger units with a fully maintained program the duties would include at least the following responsibilities:

* Identify risk management problem areas, recommend corrective action.

* Prepare risk management budget, including insurance, safety, and loss prevention controls.

* Stay informed of local, state, and federal court decisions, rules and regulations, and statutes.

* Establish, maintain, and supervise an agency-wide program of employee safety and loss prevention.

* Establish claims reporting and maintaining procedures.

* Keep administrative staff and governing body informed.

* Work with legal counsel and insurance broker to constantly monitor, supervise, and administer the overall program.

* Establish insurance requirements for vendors and contractors doing business with the agency and approve all contracts regarding compliance with requirements.

The key point to remember is that it must be someone's responsibility or it ends up being no one's obligation. The adminstrator's role doesn't end with the appointment of a risk management officer. One must be willing to release proper authority allowing the officer to carry out such duties as initiating safety meetings, training programs, inspections, investigations, and general supervision of the program. The successful administrator will make a statement of responsibility by:
• establishing goals,
• assigning responsibility,
• releasing authority,
• encouraging feedback, and
• monitoring progress.

Supervisors play a vital role in risk management planning and execution. The supervisor generally has the most influence and control over employee work habits and attitudes. The "on-site" supervisor is familiar with the day-to-day work environment and is in a critical position to affect the outcome of any risk management plan.

Management's challenge is to involve supervisory staff in a total commitment to safety and risk management -- a commitment that stems from understanding and belief in the value of such a system. The personal support of an enthusiastic supervisor spurs the "action" that takes any program beyond the paper.

Finally, in the hierarchy of involvement, all employees below the supervisory level, that is *volunteers,* users, consumers, and participants, must be included in the process of developing a risk management plan.

Employees are credited with being the first to recognize on-the-job hazards. Their work brings them in daily contact with any potentially dangerous facilities or equipment, and they should be praised

31

for frequently having excellent suggestions for improving or correcting an unsafe condition.

It is not always easy to capitalize on employee skills and knowledges. Unless they understand "what's in it for them" and become committed in the same manner as their supervisors, they could perceive the new wave of regulations as just another top-down obligation imposed by the administration. They could care less! Meaningful involvement of administrators and supervisors could be the elixir that stimulates other employees to join the effort.

In developing a comprehensive risk management plan, the volunteers in particular must be part of the process. As we have learned earlier, volunteers are subject to legal actions against them in a manner similar to regular paid employees. It is important to treat volunteers as an integral part of the staff. Certification of coaches and leaders in their areas of specialty is an important aspect of risk management.

You can add credibility to your risk management plan by asking for input from your volunteers and consumers. Invite volunteers to join some of the task forces working on the project and involve consumers through telephone surveys, questionnaires, or personal interviews. Any plan encouraging such techniques will be strengthened.

DEVELOPING THE PLAN

It is virtually impossible to design a plan comprehensive enough to serve all purposes. It would be foolhardy to think that if each step is followed precisely, there will be no tort liability. The system doesn't work that way. What we are saying is that the courts have, over time, looked favorably upon certain management practices in tort liability cases. There is nothing magic about this plan. Many departments are already practicing the various tasks described, perhaps without realizing that they may already have a plan. In that case, the outline will allow you to review your current practices and improve wherever possible. For those initiating a comprehensive plan, the outline will allow for the logical sequencing of events so that you may say this is our approach to managing risk, our plan if you will, to act responsibly.

SIXTEEN STEPS TO MANAGING RISK
1. Philosophy/Policy Statements
2. Needs Assessment
3. Goals and Objectives
4. Site and Facility Development
5. Program Development
6. Supervision
7. Establishment of Rules, Regulations, Procedures
8. Safety Inspections and Investigations
9. Accident Reporting and Analysis
10. Emergency Procedures

11. Releases, Waivers, Agreements to Participate

12. Methods of Insuring Against Risk

13. In-Service Training

14. Public Relations

15. Outside Specialists, Legal/Insurance

16. Periodic Review

STEP 1. PHILOSOPHY AND POLICY STATEMENTS

Task. Develop philosophical and policy statements regarding your organization's belief in developing a risk management loss prevention and control program. This is the opportunity for the governing authority to get involved and stay involved. The governing authority should express its commitment by adopting a philosophy of risk management and by approving policy statements as they are developed.

Philosophy defined. A critical examination of the grounds for fundamental beliefs and an analysis of the basic concepts employed in the expression of such beliefs. (Webster's 3rd Int'l. Dictionary)

Suggested approach.

1. Review your existing philosophical statements found in ordinances, charters, master plans, and administrative manuals.

2. Key words to consider:
   - aim or purpose
   - qualified leaders
   - services
   - endorsement
   - commitment
   - reasonable care

3. Formulate your ideas into a specific statement related to managing risk.

4. Have your governing authority formally adopt the statement.

Sample philosophy. It is the basic purpose of the _____ to establish, improve, manage, finance, operate, and maintain a comprehensive park and recreation system. We are committed to a philosophy that will provide these services at the highest level possible. We pledge our support to using only qualified and trained leaders in accord with the best and most reasonable standard of care possible. To that end we endorse the establishment and maintenance of an extensive program to manage risk safely within the organization.

Policy defined. A definite course or method of action to guide and determine present and future decisions.

Suggested approach. It is desirable, in fact essential, to have written policies and procedures for reporting accidents, conducting field trips, establishing what records to keep, what fees and charges will be made, who must register, etc.

In developing policies, the governing authority should adopt a brief policy statement of a general nature as the basis for formulating a policy and ask the administrative staff to develop detailed guidelines for their approval.

Example. A general policy statement might be as follows: "It is the policy of _____ to require parental permission slips for all youth programs." The staff then develops specific plans for the governing authority's approval.

<u>How to Proceed</u>

* Ask a committee of your governing board or administrative staff or some combination of the two to draft a statement for review.

* Appoint a risk manager (coordinator) on a temporary or permanent basis and ask this person to prepare a draft.

* Seek advice of your legal counsel, your insurance broker, or individuals with special knowledge such as a risk manager for a local industry.

* Adopt a provisional statement and modify it later as your knowledge of risk management grows.

* Collect and assemble existing philosophical and policy statements. Review board minutes and master plans for previously adopted statements.

* Write your philosophy and policy statement.

STEP 2. NEEDS ASSESSMENT

<u>Task</u>. Take a critical look at your current risk management practices using these sixteen steps to managing risk as a guide.

NOTE: It would be a rare exception if you did not already have many items on the outline in place. What may be different for you is the overall systematic, step by step analysis of your strengths and weaknesses.

<u>Suggested approach</u>.

1. Form a task force headed by your risk management coordinator or a key administrator to review your current situation.

2. Use the following check list (Figure 4) to do a preliminary analysis of your risk management program.

3. Determine where your strengths and weaknesses appear on the checklist.

4. Develop a work program based on weaknesses by assigning task force members to specific problem areas. Use STEP 3, Goals and Objectives, for establishing reasonable time frames.

STEP 3. GOALS AND OBJECTIVES

<u>Task</u>. Develop a series of goals and objectives that will give direction and establish time frames for completing specific tasks.

<u>Goal defined</u>. The end toward which effort or ambition is directed, something to strive for.

<u>Objective defined</u>. Specific short-term projects that lead toward goal completion.

<u>Suggested approach</u>.

1. Review current goals and objectives to determine:
   A. Which ones apply to risk management.
   B. Which ones can be adopted.
   C. Check current goals and objectives against risk management outline p. 32, to determine deficiencies, establish new list of goals and objectives.

2. If goals and objectives are nonexistent, review risk management outline, assign teams to develop goals and objectives for specific areas of interest to them.

34

FIGURE 4.

PRELIMINARY SIXTEEN-STEP CHECKLIST.

	Presently identified		Written documentation		Need improvement		Will be completed by (___ Date)	Actually completed by (___ Date)
	Yes	No	Yes	No	Yes	No		
1. Philosophy/Policy								
2. Needs Assessment								
3. Goals and Objectives								
4. Site and Facility Development								
5. Program Development								
6. Supervision								
7. Establishment of Rules, Regulations, Procedures								
8. Safety Inspections and Investigations								
9. Accident Reporting and Analysis								
10. Emergency Procedures								
11. Releases, Waivers, Agreements to Participate								
12. Methods of Insuring Against Risk								
13. In-service Training								
14. Public Relations								
15. Outside Specialists, Legal/Insurance								
16. Peridoc Review								

Samples.

Goals: To develop a comprehensive risk management plan that will encompass all departmental operations.

Objective: 1. By the end of (specify month) secure policy direction from governing authority regarding the development of a risk management plan.

2. By (specify time) appoint a risk management coordinator.

3. Inform entire staff by (specify time) of the development of a comprehensive risk management plan.

Goal: _____

_____

_____

_____

_____

Objectives: _____

_____

_____

_____

_____

NOTE: Each part of the risk management outline will need its own set of objectives with specific time frames. Experience has shown that employees who help create their own goals and objectives are more apt to carry them out. It is well worth the effort to involve staff rather than to impose goals and objectives on them.

STEP 4. SITE AND FACILITY DEVELOPMENT

Task. In the planning, layout, design, and construction of sites and physical facilities it is important to work closely with architects, engineers, program specialists, landscape architects, and builders to assure:

* Elimination of all potential site and building hazards

* Conformance to building codes

* Conformance to national, state, and local standards including size, layout, health, fire, emergency, and building codes

* Functional, aesthetically pleasing facilities.

Suggested approach.

1. Review current site and facility development projects and make a list of desirable practices from previous developments plus a similar list of undesirable experiences to avoid.

36

2. Inform architects, planners, and designers of your intent to be involved as part of the team.

3. Like all professionals, architects, planners, and designers cannot work in a vacuum. Tell them what you and your staff want and what you will and will not accept. If you expect the facility to meet national competitive standards, say so up front.

4. Include your board, staff, and the public in the process. It is human nature to be supportive of something you have been involved in from the beginning.

Develop specific reporting sheets for each site and facility. Be certain to include the following types of information.

Identify facility: _____

Date of review: _____

Specific use of the facility: _____

Potential hazards (date)	Identified (date)	Eliminated
1.		
2.		
3.		
4.		
5.		

NOTE: Sample checklists are attached in the Appendix.

STEP 5. PROGRAM DEVELOPMENT

Task. It is your obligation to provide consumers with quality recreation experiences, professionally taught according to acceptable standards. You have a duty to protect your governing authority, your staff, and volunteers by adhering to a program based upon the following approaches:

Suggested approach.
1. Activities should be taught by qualified personnel. Instructors, including volunteers, should demonstrate certifiable qualifications. If the volunteers are not trained, it is your responsibility to require training appropriate to the task.

2. Require instructors to teach progressively in keeping with the principles of human development and in accord with the participant's skill and experience levels.

3. Provide sufficient numbers of leaders for the program, equipment, and areas used.

4. Point out potential dangers to the participants and parents. Be specific and straightforward, require releases, waivers, or agreements to participate where necessary.

37

5. Keep records on file including but not limited to:

* Instructor qualification	* Medical examination clearances
* Evaluations	* Safety instruction
* Lesson plans	* Eligibility requirements
* Schedules	* Manuals of operation
* Emergency procedures	* Reports for accident, injury, or incident
* Release/waivers	* Agreements to participate

6. Make certain each program has been authorized by the administration and governing authority.

It is essential that the governing authority give credence to activities, field trips, etc., in the form of a policy statement.

1. We _____ hereby authorize our staff to offer programs in _____
  (name of authority)   (specify programs)

_____

_____

2. We _____ hereby authorize field trips as an integral part of our program
  (name of authority)
offerings.

STEP 6. SUPERVISION

Task. Develop a plan of supervision encompassing your earlier described philosophy of providing quality programs with the best and most reasonable standard of care.

Suggested approach. Identify and inform the staff of the philosophy of the organization with emphasis on the standard of care.

* Interpret the aims, objectives and policies of the organization.

* Act as a liaison between staff and administrators.

* Aid in formulating and interpreting job descriptions.

* Assist with plans for specific programs, budgets, or facilities.

* Evaluate the progress of staff and programs.

* Build creative human relationships.

* Identify activity, location, and staff participation ratios.

* Guide staff to attain expected accomplishments including:
  • Knowledge of self and others
  • The "why" of the program
  • Step-by-step procedure of visualizing, planning, organizing, assigning, and following through
  • Ability to encourage initiative
  • Ability to work democratically
  • Ability to observe and be sensitive

- Ability to make decisions
- Ability to communicate
- Ability to act and react
- Awareness of emergency procedures
- Knowledge of surroundings and consciousness of participant's physical condition, fatigue, or heat exhaustion
- Alertness to environmental changes due to weather, including snow, wind, rain, lightning

NOTE: Remember: if employees, including volunteers, claim to be qualified, they should be prepared to provide a standard of care in keeping with that of a reasonable and prudent professional. if you as an administrator or supervisor are aware of incompetent employees or volunteers and choose to do nothing about it, you too could be implicated if legal action is taken against such individuals.

See appendix for supervisor's evaluation form.

Plan of Supervision

Goal: Prepare a written plan of supervision for each site, facility, and program component.

Example: Using a swimming pool as an example, a plan of supervision would include but not be limited to:

1. Qualifications of staff
2. Documented proof of current staff qualifications
3. Written and signed job descriptions
4. Documented evaluations of performance
5. In-service training schedules, including outlines of material covered
6. Documented standards for pool capacity
7. Documented standards for ratio of lifeguards to swimmers
8. Documented plan showing lifeguard stations, areas of supervision, rotation schedules, specific danger areas, etc.
9. Water clarity and purification standards
10. Posted emergency procedures
11. Documented proof of in-service training for emergencies
12. Written lesson plans for all skill levels
13. Safety check lists including:

- pool deck
- change rooms
- showers
- office
- first aid kits
- emergency alarm
- rescue equipment
- water testing
- deep water lifelines
- outside grounds
- gates and fences
- aquatic staff room
- diving boards
- backwash schedule
- posted rules and regulations
- electrical equipment
- chemical equipment and storage
- doors and windows locked

NOTE: If called to testify in a liability case, there is nothing as comforting as having a carefully documented proof of your supervisory techniques.

<u>Task</u>. Assemble all the safety rules and regulations pertaining to program services and the procedures used to enforce them.

<u>Suggested approach</u>.

1. Identify all the safety rules and regulations that should be included in this file, including:
    * Rules and regulations that have been established for use of parks, picnic areas and shelters, community rooms, buildings and equipment.
    * Rules for golf courses, pools, beaches, tennis facilities, ice rinks, marinas, boat usage, and other aquatic equipment.
    * Rules and regulations for use of arts and crafts facilities and equipment.

2. Review all program areas for safety rules and regulations and add to the above list.

3. Establish reporting and record keeping procedures to monitor the system; update and revise as necessary.

4. Review all signage throughout your system. A complete analysis of all signs, informational, directional, warning, and so forth, should become a regular part of a risk management program.

5. While the above rules and regulations are aimed at the consumers of your programs, it is equally important to monitor a complete safety program for employees. (See note.)

NOTE: While the author recognizes the importance of assuring a safe and healthful working environment for employees and the necessity to encourage employers and employees to reduce hazards in the workplace, this publication is primarily aimed at managing risk for the consumer of activities rather than the providers.

Reference is made to the Occupational Safety and Health Act (OSH-ACT) and NIOSH, the National Institute for Occupational Safety and Health. NIOSH was established under the OSH Act but unlike ASHA, which is under the Department of Labor, NIOSH is in the Department of Health and Human Services. All aspects of OSHA and NIOSH plus state mandates should be integrated into the risk management plan. See Appendix for additional information about OSHA.

<u>Safety Rules and Regulations</u>.

Identify in a general way all the facilities, areas, programs, and equipment for which you have established rules, regulations, and procedures. These include:

Parks	Water-related facilities
Recreation centers	Woodlands
Golf courses	Trails
Playgrounds	Camps
_____	_____
_____	_____
_____	_____
_____	_____

Take each general area and identify specific rules and regulations for that facility and/or program. For example: water-related facilities.

Facilities	Programs
Pools - indoor-outdoor	Swimming lessons
Beaches	Lifeguard training
Lakes	Swim teams
Ponds	General open swimming
Rivers	Scuba lessons
Streams	Boating
Water falls	Sailing
Canals	Wind surfing
	Canoeing

_____   _____

_____   _____

_____   _____

CAVEAT: Rules and regulations are only as good as your enforcement procedures. If rules and regulations are advertised and not enforced, it could be interpreted as a breach of duty (nonfeasance or misfeasance) on the part of the managing authority and its employees.

STEP 8. SAFETY INSPECTIONS AND INVESTIGATIONS

Task. Develop a routine, systematic method for safety inspections and investigations.

Suggested approach.

1. Determine what is to be inspected and how frequently. It is your duty to inspect and maintain.

2. Regularity is essential. Conditions change quickly and details are soon forgotten.

3. Establish a regular pattern of inspections and demand that it be kept.

4. Develop a series of checklists suitable for easy application throughout the system. For example, a playground equipment checklist can be made flexible enough to accommodate all similar facilities. Inspection sheets should reflect manufacturer's recommendations for inspections plus all national, state, and local standards if any.

5. Establish a method of reporting faulty equipment and maintenance problems that allows minimum down-time and maximum follow-up.

6. Develop a reporting and monitoring system that will allow easy access to vital statistics regarding breakdowns. When, where, why, and how often are some of the questions needing answers.

7. Investigations will depend on frequency and severity of damages and/or breakdowns.

NOTE: See Appendix for sample forms.

Safety Inspections

Title of inspection checklists	In use yes no	Needs up dating yes no	To be developed yes no
1. Playground equipment	__ __	__ __	__ __
2. Building inspection - interior	__ __	__ __	__ __
3. Building inspection - exterior	__ __	__ __	__ __
4. _____	__ __	__ __	__ __
5. _____	__ __	__ __	__ __
6. _____	__ __	__ __	__ __
7. _____	__ __	__ __	__ __
8. _____	__ __	__ __	__ __
9. _____	__ __	__ __	__ __

Schedule or dates for periodic inspections	Frequency of inspection
1. Playground equipment	_____
2. Building inspection - interior	_____
3. Building inspection - exterior	_____
4. _____	_____
5. _____	_____
6. _____	_____
7. _____	_____
8. _____	_____

HINT: A calendar of inspection schedules is evidence of reasonable care.

NOTE: Check with your state safety board for required inspections for items such as fire equipment, elevators. Consult with your insurance broker for advice and recommendations.

STEP 9. ACCIDENT REPORTING AND ANALYSIS

Task. Our primary goal should be to report the facts in an objective and unbiased manner and in sufficient detail to allow for analysis and appraisal.

Suggested approach. Compare your accident report forms with the examples in the Appendix. List any ideas for changes below and revise your form accordingly.

1. The written report must be completed with extreme care, since it could be used as evidence in a suit brought against you and your governing authority.

DO NOT ASK FOR OR RECORD OPINIONS AND COMMENTS ABOUT HOW SUCH AN ACCIDENT MIGHT BE PREVENTED IN THE FUTURE!

2. Establish a system for recording and monitoring all accidents. You will want to know how often and where accidents occur, the severity of the accident, time of day, and whether of not the activity was supervised or unsupervised. This information will allow staff to analyze frequencies and possible patterns and to make necessary adjustments in programs, equipment, or supervision.

NOTE: See Appendix for sample accident report forms.

Accident reporting

Record your ideas for updating your accident report form here.

1. _____
2. _____
3. _____
4. _____
5. _____
6. _____
7. _____
8. _____
9. _____
10. _____

STEP 10. EMERGENCY PROCEDURES

Task. Develop a procedure for handling emergencies and adapt it to all settings.

Consider the following:

* Require first aid and CPR training for all staff, full and part-time. It is your responsibility as an employer to pay for this on-the-job training during working hours.

* Require medical information sheets for high-risk activities, contact sports, adventure trips, and older American centers.

* Locate first aid kits in all department vehicles.

* Develop a schedule for checking and re-stocking first aid equipment.

* Provide emergency procedure instruction sheets in each first aid kit.

* Make arrangements for emergency phone use in out-of-the-way areas.

* Be particularly aware of emergency procedures during special events and any large gatherings. Consult with local EMTs and others providing emergency services.

* Establish emergency evacuation plans for all facilities.

* Provide occupational illness and injury control methods and physicals for employees.

* Add your own particular interests and needs to this list.

NOTE: Emergencies can by their very nature vary from a playground accident to a sudden tornado or windstorm. They are virtually impossible to predict. It is also impossible to know how our leaders and supervisors will respond under emergency conditions. The trauma normally connected with emergencies can be substantially reduced by having an emergency plan that is well documented and has become second nature for all employees through proper indoctrination and training.

1. Assign a task force to review all current policies.

2. Ask for assistance from local professionals: EMTs, paramedics, hospitals, doctors, emergency squad personnel, police and fire departments, clinics, anyone who may be in a position to assist you in developing and/or improving your emergency program.

STEP 11. RELEASES, WAIVERS, AGREEMENTS TO PARTICIPATE

Task. Analyze your current program in light of the latest information available and make adjustments where necessary.

Suggested approach.

1. Review your present philosophy toward the use of releases, waivers, and agreements to participate.
   * Why do you use them? Why not?
   * How are they being used? By whom?
   * Where are they kept on file? For how long?

2. With the assistance of legal counsel, review all documents in current use.
   * Is language sufficient for your jurisdiction?
   * Is language explicit enough?
   * Seek advice regarding statute of limitations in your jurisdiction.

3. Check with professional colleagues for their ideas on the topic and ask for samples of their forms.

4. Use the samples found in the Appendix for ideas and share them with your legal counsel and staff.

5. Be sure to have your governing authority approve all new and/or revised policies.

6. Finally, develop or revise your forms, including a written procedure for the use of each form. Document where each is filed and the location of the permanent record file.

Notes for developing your forms

STEP 12. *METHODS OF INSURING AGAINST RISK*

Task. Identify the alternatives available for your jurisdiction and select the best combination that will allow the most cost effective protection.

Suggested approach.

1. Consult with your legal and insurance counselors. See Step 15, p.

2. Understand enough of the language in order to communicate effectively. The most common loss protection methods are:

   a. Avoidance. Simply do away with all park, recreation, and leisure service programs. It is just as futile to assume you can avoid liability problems by assuming a perfect world where all activities are conducted properly and all participant's behave admirably.

   b. Reduction. This is what this plan is all about: reduce your losses by planning, organizing, training, and controlling as many contingencies as possible.

   c. Retention. Retain the risk by self-insured. This is, in effect, no coverage at all.

   d. Transference. Have others carry the risk: individual and family insurance, leasing, contracting, purchase insurance, surety bonds, use waivers, hold harmless clauses, agreements to participate. Assist staff in aquiring personal liability coverage and encourage participants to carry insurance certificates.

Figure 5. A Check List of Insurance Coverages.

1. Do you have insurance covering the following?

   a) Comprehensive general liability
   Yes   If yes, company
      Policy #   Date Expires
      Agent   Phone #
   No   If no, why?

   b) Fire and extended coverage
   Yes   If yes, company
      Policy #   Date Expires
      Agent   Phone #
   No   If no, why?

   c) Workers compensation
   Yes   If yes, company
      Policy #   Date Expires
      Agent   Phone #
   No   If no, why?

   d) Property and equipment damage
   Yes   If yes, company
      Policy #   Date Expires
      Agent   Phone #
   No   If no, why?

   e) Vehicle liability, collision, etc.
   Yes   If yes, company
      Policy #   Date Expires
         Agent   Phone #
   No   If no, why?

   f) Non-owners's vehicle liability
   Yes   If yes, company
         Policy #   Date Expires
         Agent   Phone #
   No   If no, why?

   g) Umbrella catastrophe
   Yes   If yes, company
         Policy #   Date Expires
         Agent   Phone #
   No   If no, why?

   h) Hired or leased vehicles
   Yes   If yes, company
         Policy #   Date Expires
         Agent   Phone #
   No   If no, why?

45

i) Unemployment compensation
   Yes   If yes, company
        Policy #   Date Expires
        Agent   Phone #
   No   If no, why?

j) Participant's accident and illness
   Yes   If yes, company
        Policy #   Date Expires
        Agent   Phone #
   No   If no, why?

k) Staff negligence
   Yes   If yes, company
        Policy #   Date Expires
        Agent   Phone #
   No   If no, why?

l) Medical malpractice
   Yes   If yes, company
   Policy #   Date Expires
        Agent   Phone #
   No   If no, why?

m) Officer's and director's liability
   Yes   If yes, company
        Policy #   Date Expires
   Agent   Phone #
   No   If no, why?

n) False advertising
   Yes   If yes, company
        Policy #   Date Expires
        Agent   Phone #
   No   If no, why?

o) Early closure and tuition refund
   Yes   If yes, company
        Policy #   Date Expires
        Agent   Phone #
   No   If no, why?

p) Product liability
   Yes   If yes, company
        Policy #   Date Expires
        Agent   Phone #
   No   If no, why?

q) Bonding
   Yes   If yes, company
        Policy #   Date Expires
   Agent   Phone #
   No   If no, why?

r) Specific high-risk program activities
   Yes   If yes, company
        Policy   Date Expires
        Agent   Phone #
   No   If no, why?

s) Personal effects of participants and/or staff
   Yes   If yes, company
        Policy #   Date Expires
        Agent   Phone #
   No   If no, why?

Others

2. Who may contact the insurance agent and in what circumstances?

3. Where are insurance policies filed? Who has access?

4. Where are claim forms kept? Who may file a claim?

STEP 13. IN-SERVICE TRAINING

 Task. Develop a comprehensive program of in-service training for the entire staff, including members of the governing authority and volunteers.

 Suggested approach.

1. Identify within your system who will be trained and develop groups with some commonalities. For example:
   • Board/commission or corporate members
   • Administrators
   • Supervisors
   • Program leaders
   • Foremen
   • Office personnel
   • Laborers
   • Volunteers

2. Develop as many training groups as necessary to accommodate your operation.

3. Develop goals and objectives with the help of your task force for training each group identified above.

Sample In-Service Training Procedure

Audience: Board/commission and/or corporate members.

Goal: To have each board/commission and/or corporate member knowledgeable of all major aspects of the system.

Objectives: Within the first three months of their term, acquaint each new board member with the following:

1. Legal provisions, authority to operate, provisions of governing statutes, or corporate by-laws.

2. Department policy statements, objectives, history.

3. Board duties and responsibilities.

4. Powers and duties of chief executive.

5. Organizational structure.

6. Personnel policies and practices.

7. List of staff names and positions.

8. List of facilities, including size, type, location, etc.

9. Provisions governing finances, planning, programs, public relations.

10. Procedure for managing risk within the organization.

Audience: Administrators

Goal:

Objectives:

STEP 14. PUBLIC RELATIONS

Task. In this context, public relations means working within the entire system to get the work out about your pro-active philosophy of managing risk and identifying your method of following up on all risk-related activities.

Suggested approach.

1. Your risk management plan, when adopted, will provide a practical and philosophical base for building a solid public relations program.

2. The fact that you have adopted a pro-active approach to managing risk will begin to show up in program brochures, news releases, audio/visual presentations, speeches, staff meetings, in-service training programs, wherever your department is discussed.

3. Public relations means:
   * Having informed, visible staff
   * Being nice to people
   * Consistency of rule enforcement
   * Treating users as family
   * Well-kept and maintained areas and facilities
   * Using waivers, releases, agreement to participate
   * Employing only qualified personnel
   * How to handle the news media

4. There is no substitute for showing genuine concern for an injured party after the accident. A good public relations program and follow-up can often dissolve bitter and unhappy feelings that may lead to unnecessary litigation. There are, however, differences of philosophy on what department personnel should do following an accident. Should you visit or call on the injured party expressing concern and best wishes or do you ignore all contact and follow-up to avoid possible self-incrimination? Discuss this with your legal counsel and insurance underwriter, determine a plan, and administer it consistently.

Public Relations

Our plan:

STEP 15. OUTSIDE SPECIALISTS - - LEGAL/INSURANCE

Task. Contact and have available competent legal and insurance counselors.

Suggested approach.

1. It is not unusual for public agencies either to have their own legal counsel, usually on a retainer basis, or to have access to such counsel through the city/county/state legal department. Whatever method is available to you, it is very important to be on a first-name basis with those professionals you depend on for legal counsel.

2. For private, semi-private, or commercial agencies or corporations, it is just as critical to have access to appropriate legal counsel - - someone you can depend on for competent advice and service when needed.

3. The same suggestions hold for insurance counselors. There is no substitute for good advice when it comes to using professional insurance counselors. They can and should take the guesswork out of helping you plan your insurance needs.

Legal/Insurance Specialists

Legal contact	Insurance contact
_____	_____
_____	_____
_____	_____
_____	_____
_____	_____

STEP 16. PERIODIC REVIEW

Task. Establish review procedures, a timetable, and have documented evidence that verifies your good intentions.

Suggested approach.

1. Consider various parts of this plan from the viewpoint of frequency of review. Certain areas will obviously stand out. For example, insurance by its very nature must be reviewed frequently. Other areas such as safety inspections and investigations, accident reporting and analysis, emergency procedures, releases, waivers, and agreements to participate can be put on a regular schedule of review.

2. Use the first fifteen steps of this plan as a checklist to make certain you are touching all the bases.

3. Be able to show evidence that you do, in fact, take your obligation to manage risk very seriously.

Periodic Review

First review date: _____

Procedure:

BIBLIOGRAPHY

1. A Handbook for Public Playground Safety, Volume I: General Guidelines for New and Existing Playgrounds, U.S. Consumer Product Safety Commission, Washington, DC, 1981.

2. A Handbook for Public Playground Safety, Volume II: Technical Guidelines for Equipment and Surfacing, U.S. Consumer Product Safety Commission, Washington DC, 1981.

3. Appenzeller, Herb and Appenzeller, Thomas, Sports and the Courts, The Michie Company, Charlottesville, VA, 1980.

4. Appenzeller, Herb, Physical Education and the Law, The Michie Company, Charlottesville, VA, 1978.

5. Berry, Robert C., and Wong, Glen M., Law and Business of the Sports Industries, Auburn House Publishing Company, Dover, MA, 1986.

6. Connors, Eugene T., Educational Tort Liability and Malpractice, Phi Delta Kappa, Bloomington, IN, 1981.

7. Decof, Leonard, and Godosky, Richard, Sports Injury Litigation, Practicing Law Institute, 1979.

8. Frakt, Arthur N., and Rankin, Janna S., The Law of Parks, Recreation Resources and Leisure Services, Brighton Publishing Co., Salt Lake City, UT, 1982.

9. Grimaldi, John V., and Simonds, Rollin H., Safety Management, 3rd Edition, Richard D. Irwin, Inc., Homewood, IL, 1975.

10. Heinrich, H. W., Petersen, Dan, and Roos, Nestor, Industrial Accident Prevention, McGraw-Hill Book Company, New York, 1980.

11. Judd, Richard L., and Ponsell, Dwight D., The First Responder, C. V. Mosby Company, St. Louis, MO, 1982.

12. Kaiser, Ronald A., Liability and Law in Recreation, Parks, and Sports, Prentice-Hall, Englewood Cliffs, NJ, 1986.

13. Kozlowski, James C., Recreation and Parks Law Reporter Quarterly, National Recreation and Park Association, Alexandria, VA, 1986.

14. Nygaard, Gary, and Boone, Thomas H., Coaches Guide to Sports Law, Human Kinetics Publishers, Champaign, IL, 1985.

15. Nygaard, Gary, and Boone, Thomas H., The Law for Physical Educators and Coaches, Brighton Publishing Co., Salt Lake City, UT, 1981.

16. Shivers, Jay S., Recreational Safety, Associated University Presses, Inc., Cranbury, NJ, 1986.

17. Stern, James F., and Hendry, Earl R., Swimming Pools and the Law, S. & H. Books, Milwaukee, 1977.

18. Townley, Stephen, and Grayson, Edward, Sponsorship of Sports, Arts, and Leisure: Law, Tax, and Business Relationships, Sweet and Maxwell, London, 1984.

19. Valente, Paula R., Current Approaches to Risk Management: A Directory of Practices, International City Management Association, Washington, DC, 1980.

20. van der Smissen, Betty, Legal Liability of Cities and Schools for Injuries in Recreation and Parks, The W. H. Anderson Company, Cincinnati, OH, 1968.

21. Wasserman, Natalie, and Phelus, Dean G., Editors, Risk Management Today: A How-to-Guide for Local Government, International City Management Association, Washington, DC, 1985.

22. Weistart, John C., and Lowell, Cym H., The Law of Sports, the Bobbs-Merrill Company, Inc., Indianapolis, IN, 1979.

23. Yasser, Ray, Sports Law, University Press of America, Inc., Lanham, MD, 1985.

APPENDICES

These appendices were reprinted with permission from the following agencies:

    Bensenville Park District, Bensenville, IL
    Bloomington Department of Parks and Recreation, Bloomington, IN
    Buffalo Grove Park District, Buffalo Grove, IL
    Champaign Park District, Champaign, IL
    City of Kettering Parks and Recreation Department, Kettering, OH
    City of Woodstock, Recreation Division, Woodstock, IL
    Department of Parks and Recreation, Redmond, VA
    Department of Parks and Recreation, Topeka, KS
    Department of Parks and Recreation,Worthington, OH
    Department of Parks, Recreation and Properties, Cleveland, OH
    Department of Parks, Recreation and Public Lands, Billings, MT
    Jackson County Parks and Recreation, Blue Springs, MO
    Johnson County Park and Recreation District, Shawnee Mission, KS
    Niles Park District, Niles, IL
    Parks and Recreation Board, Maple Grove, MN
    Parks and Recreation Department, Sun Prarie, WI
    Parks and Recreation Services Division, Eugene, OR
    Prentice-Hall, Inc, Englewood Cliffs, NJ
    Suburban Hennepin Regional Park District, Plymouth, MN
    Urbana Park District, Urbana, IL

APPENDIX A

POLICY STATEMENTS, INDEMNIFICATION, SAFETY COMMITTEE

RISK MANAGEMENT POLICY STATEMENTS

RELEASE DATE: October 8, 19
REPLACES ISSUE DATED:

DEPARTMENT RESPONSIBLE: Management Services

Policy

The following Risk Management Policy Statement was adopted by the Park District's Board of Commissioners on January 2, 1986.

The Suburban Hennepin Regional Park District desires to protect itself against accidental losses, which in the aggregate during any Financial period may significantly affect Park District personnel, property, its budget, or ability to fulfill its responsibilities.

The Park District resolves that any loss of life or serious personal injury to employees or members of the general public are unacceptable.

The Park District will manage its risks of accidental loss by applying a process that includes the following:

o A systematic and continuous identification of loss exposure;
o An analysis of these exposures in terms of frequency and severity;
o The application of sound loss prevention and loss procedures;
o Ongoing review of available and economically beneficial risk transfer alternatives; and
o The retention of self-funding of the risk consistent with the Park District's financial resources and statutory obligations.

General Information

Implementation of an effective Risk Management Program is predicated on establishing clear and concise policy direction. The Risk Manager policy statement provides a broad policy that clearly states the Board's intent with respect to risk management. The policy is amplified and made operational through administrative statements and procedures such as the Loss Prevention Statement and the Work Related Injury Control Statement.

Procedure

Loss Prevention Statement/ Safety Committee

SUBURBAN HENNEPIN REGIONAL PARK DISTRICT having gone on record as promoting a Risk Management Policy which will prevent the loss of life or serious personal injury to employees or members of the general public, resolves that:

IT SHALL BE EACH EMPLOYEE'S RESPONSIBILITY TO BE AWARE OF HIS/HER SURROUNDINGS SO AS TO TAKE NOTICE OF ANY UNSAFE ACT OR CONDITION. THESE SITUATIONS SHALL BE BROUGHT TO THE ATTENTION OF THAT PERSON'S IMMEDIATE SUPERVISOR FOR CORRECTIVE ACTION.

In order to facilitate a loss prevention program within the Park District a safety committee comprised of staff from throughout the Park District shall be established to:

o Assist in developing safe work habits and safety conscious attitudes;
o Help identify and focus attention on specific causes of accidents;
o Prepare recommendations for primary and supplemental safety training;
o Provide a forum for employees to participate in accident prevention activities;
o Provide a channel of communication between workers and management;
o Improve employee and public relations;
o Help reduce the frequency and seriousness of accidents of employees and park visitors.

The Park District Safety Committee is chaired by the District Maintenance Manager. Specific safety concerns may be addressed to the Chair or other Committee members. The Committee's operational guidelines, reporting forms, etc., are available through the Committee Chair. If, for any reasons, the employee feels that the Park District has not properly responded to a safety concern, this should be brought to the attention of the Park District's Risk Manager, who is charged with administration and coordination of the Park District's overall safety program.

Work Related Injury Control Statement

Once a work related injury has occurred, a number of actions should be taken in the following order:

o The injured party should be attended to immediately.

In case of serious injury, the injured person should be transported to the closest hospital by ambulance or other emergency vehicle. (Call 911)

In case of all other work related injuries including back injury, sprains, hernias, etc., the injured party can be sent or taken to one of the following clinics:

    North Memorial Hospital
    Apple Valley Clinic
    Group Health, Inc.

o In all cases, someone other than the injured party shall call ahead to the medical facility being used to make them aware of the situation.

o In all cases, the injured person shall report the loss to his/her supervisor immediately. The supervisor shall complete the first report of injury form and send it to the Park District's Personnel Assistant.

THE INJURED PARTY MUST REPORT THE LOSS WHEN IT OCCURS. THE SUPERVISOR MUST SEND A REPORT TO THE PERSONNEL ASSISTANT THE SAME DAY THE LOSS OCCURS. ADDITIONS OR CLARIFICATIONS CAN BE MADE AT A LATER DATE.

The loss report shall be sent to the Workers Compensation insurance company. A copy will be sent to the Park District's Risk Manager and a copy will be filed for the OSHA report log.

o When a permanent or seasonal employee is
  injured on the job, s/he will be granted
  authorized paid time off on the day of claimed
  injury, without deduction from leave balances,
  to secure needed medical attention from a
  Hennepin Parks designated medical facility.
  Paid time off will include travel time to and
  from the medical facility, time spent at the
  medical facility for treatment, and time off
  for the remainder of that workday if the
  employee is sent home by the medical
  authority. Such paid time off will not exceed
  the hours remaining in that employee's
  scheduled work shift for the day of injury.

o Each injured employee shall be contacted
  periodically by his/her immediate supervisor.

  Any employee absent more than 3 days from work
  should be visited, in person, at least once a
  week by their respective manager or department
  head.

  Every effort shall be made by all parties to
  return an injured employee to his/her job as
  soon as possible or provide suitable light
  duty work as allowed by the attending
  physician.

EMPLOYEE INDEMNIFICATION

RELEASE DATE: October 8, 19
REPLACES ISSUE DATED:

DEPARTMENT RESPONSIBLE: Management Services

Policy

Under Minnesota Statutes 466, the Park District is authorized to defend and indemnify any of its commissioners, officers and employees against any tort claim, or demand. On February 25, 1986, the Board of Commissioners adopted a resolution providing such indemnification. This essentially reaffirmed and clarified a previous 1975 resolution.

Resolution

WHEREAS, Chapter 798, Laws of Minnesota 1963, reduced the application of the doctrine of governmental immunity with respect to municipal corporations and its employees, and

WHEREAS, employees of the Suburban Hennepin Regional Park District have been exposed to additional tort liability in the performance of their official duties; and

WHEREAS, said Chapter 798, Laws of Minnesota 1963, now coded as Minnesota Statues 1969, Chapter 466.01 through 446.15 by Section 466.07, authorized the governing body of any municipality to defend, save harmless and indemnify any of its commissioners, officers, and employees against any tort claim or demand whether groundless or otherwise arising out of an alleged act or omission occurring in the performance of a duty, except that of malfeasance in office or willful or wanton neglect of duty;

NOW, THEREFORE, BE IT RESOLVED that the Suburban Hennepin Regional Park District will defend, save harmless and indemnify any commissioner, officer, agent, employee or bona fide volunteer, whether elective or appointive, against any tort or professional liability claim or demand or claim for deprivation of a constitutional right whether groundless or otherwise arising out of an alleged act or omission occurring in the performance of duty; that the Suburban Hennepin Regional Park District may at its option compromise and/or settle any such claim or judgment and pay the amount of any settlement or judgment rendered thereon in accordance with the Suburban Hennepin Regional Park District employee tort and professional liability indemnification plan dated February 25, 1986, on file with the Secretary to the Board.

General Information

The statutes contain specific requirements for perfecting a claim against the Park District which must be followed in order for a claim to be allowable. Further, the Park District's Employee Tort and Professional Liability Indemnification Plan included as an addendum to this policy contains specific provisions which must apply before employee indemnification or defense. If claims are to be properly investigated and defended, it is essential that the Plan's provisions be observed.

Employee Tort and Professional Liability Indemnification Plan

Included as an Addendum to this policy.

SUBURBAN HENNEPIN REGIONAL PARK DISTRICT EMPLOYEE TORT AND PROFESSIONAL LIABILITY INDEMNIFICATION PLAN

I. __Declaration of Indemnification.__ Having in mind the public policy implicit in Minn. Stat. Ch. 466 (1963) to protect those performing governmental services on behalf of political subdivisions against specified risks and to protect individuals from specified injuries and damages resulting therefrom, the Suburban Hennepin Regional Park District Board of Commissioners hereby declares that the Park District will defend, save harmless and indemnify any commissioner, officer, agent, employee or volunteer, whether elective or appointive, against any tort or professional liability claim or demand, or claim for deprivation of a constitutional right, whether groundless or otherwise, arising out of an alleged act or omission occurring in the performance of duty; that the Park District may at its option compromise and settle any such claim or suit and pay the amount of any settlement or judgment rendered thereon.

II. __Definitions.__ For the purpose of this Indemnification Plan only the following definitions shall apply:

A. __Employee.__ A commissioner, officer, agent, employee, hereinafter collectively referred to as "employee," shall include all persons employed by the Park District whose pay comes in whole or in part from Park District funds and who are working under the direction or control of any official or department of the Park District. The term "employee." shall include those who work for the Park District on a voluntary basis without pay when such employment is accepted, contracted for or consented to by the Park District or a department thereof and under the direction and control of the Park District or department thereof. The term "employee" specifically excludes any person or organization contracting to perform services or act for the Park District as an independent contractor. The term "employee" shall also include any person serving with or without compensation in any form as a member of a board, task force or commission duly established by the Park District to advise on matters of policy or procedure.

B. __Performance of Duty.__ The term "performance of duty" shall be interpreted as broadly as possible to include any situation in which a Park District employee could conceivably be deemed to be acting within the scope of his employment. The term "performance of duty" shall not include any act or omission constituting criminal conduct or deliberate and intentional wrongful or unauthorized conduct or malfeasance in office or willful or wanton neglect of duty within the meaning of Minn. Stat. Chapter 466.

III. __Defense of Actions.__ As appropriate, the Park District will provide an attorney to defend any Park District employee pursuant to this Indemnification Plan. The Park District reserves the right to designate said attorney to defend an employee.

IV. Liability Limitations

A. The Park District shall indemnify any employee in the following amounts:

1. $200,000 when the claim is one for death by wrongful act or omission and $200,000 to any claimant in any other case.

2. $600,000 for any number of claims arising out of a single occurrence.

B. In any case where, by court decision or legislation, the limits of liability do not apply to the Park District or its employees, the Park District shall indemnify an employee for any amounts ordered by the court as final judgment.

C. The Park District specifically reserves any defenses which are made available to Park District or its employees.

V. Payment and Allocation of Claims. All claims to be paid as a result of the indemnification provided by this Plan may be paid from the Park District Risk Management Contingency Fund or any other fund established for these purposes. Any judgment or settlement in a claim against the Park District shall be paid in accordance with the provisions of Minn. Stat. 466.09.

VI. Cooperation of Employee. No defense or indemnification shall be provided by the Park District to any employee in any of the following circumstances:

A. If the employee fails to use diligent efforts in reporting to the employee's department head any incident which he/she might reasonably expect could result in a claim of liability against him, or the Park District.

B. If any employee fails to notify the Director of Management Services of any notice of claim or summons and complaint served upon him commencing a suit for damages reimbursable under this Plan. Such notice shall be given to the Director of Management Services within ten days of its service upon the employee.

C. If any employee refuses to cooperate with an investigation or defense of any claim or lawsuit by any attorney employed by the Park District to furnish defense to said employee, or any private investigator hired by the Park District to investigate such claim.

VII. Effect of Other Insurance, Bond or Indemnification Plan. If the Park District or employee against whom a claim or judgment reimbursable under this Plan is asserted has any other valid insurance, bond or indemnification plan available covering the loss or damage alleged against him, such insurance, bond or other plan will be primary and will be first applied to the payment of any claim or judgment. However, if the monies applied are not sufficient to pay the claim or judgment in full, the obligation of the Park District is limited to the difference between the primary payment and the "Liability Limitations" of the Park District as heretofore set forth in Paragraph IV of this Indemnification Plan.

VIII. Subrogation Rights of the Park District. In the event of any payment under this Plan, the Park District shall be subrogated to all of the employee's rights of recovery therefore against any person or organization and the employee shall execute and deliver instruments and papers and do whatever else is necessary to secure such rights. The employee shall do nothing after loss to prejudice such rights.

IX. Assignments Prohibited. Assignment of interest under this Plan is not permitted without the written consent of the Park District signed by the Chairperson of its Board of Commissioners and no such assignment shall bind the Park District unless such written consent is given prior to assignment. If, however, the employee shall die, the benefits of this Plan shall be available to and apply fully to the employee's legal representative, but only while acting within the scope of his duties as such.

X. Continuation of Protection. Any defense and indemnification available to an employee under this Plan shall continue to be available to him after the termination of his employment so long as the act or omission causing his liability occurred during the course of his duties while an employee of the Park District. Such defense and indemnification shall not be available to a former employee; however, in the event that the liability claim against him is asserted as a counterclaim or set off in any suit brought by the employee, except to the extent that the liability of such employee may exceed the amount of his own claim or suit.

XI. Effective Date. This Plan is effective beginning the ___25th___ day of _____February_____, 1986 upon Resolution of the Park District Board of Commissioners of the same date.

0325C

SAFETY COMMITTEE

OPERATING PROCEDURES

1. The Safety Committee is to meet on a monthly basis (first Thursday).

   a. The meeting date is to be determined by membership consensus.

2. The business of the Safety Committee is to discuss and help coordinate the safety and general welfare of all employees and public park users.

3. The Safety Committee is to help insure that safety training is provided for safety and general welfare of all employees and public park users.

4. The Safety Committee will work in conjunction with qualified safety experts to help insure that safety inspections are performed by qualified inspectors at Hennepin Parks facilties on an as-needed basis.

   a. In cases where the Committee determines that significant safety concerns exist, inspections will be conducted by qualified investigators.

   b. On a day-to-day basis, Safety Committee members will encourage informal inspections by all employees at their work locations, with concerns being reported to the Safety Committee.

5. The Safety Committee is to receive, analyze and monitor safety concerns submitted by any employee, volunteer, park guest or regulatory agency.

   a. All Committee members' names and work phone numbers shall be posted at all work locations for employee input.

   b. Any employee, vounteer or park guest may bring an individual concern to the attention of any Committee member.

   c. Concerns may be submitted anonymously.

   d. "Safety Committee Reviewal Request" forms shall be available for use in reporting concerns.

6. The Safety Committee shall be responsible for coordinating efforts to correct or resolve safety concerns in Hennepin Parks.

The following are guidelines for dealing with safety concerns:

a. Submitted safety concerns will be reviewed immediately by the Safety Committee Chair or designee.

b. If the concern needs immediate attention, it will be assigned to Committee members. If immediate attention is not warranted, the concern will be presented at the next scheduled Safety Committee meeting for review.

c. All concerns will be reviewed by the Committee as a whole. Each concern and any recommendation/resolution will be published in the Committee's meeting minutes.

d. Where appropriate, resolution of safety concerns will be coordinated with risk management consultants and/or other qualified experts.

e. In situations requiring major expenditures, the Committee will present its recommendations to management staff, and the risk manager consultant.

7. Safety Committee members are to represent respective groups of employees as follows:

Office Personnel:	1 member
Planning and Engineering:	1 member
Program Staff:	1 member
Rangers:	1 member
Naturalists:	1 member
Maintenance:	3 members (1 from each division)

The District Maintenance Manager and the Personnel Assistant will be permanently assigned to the Committee, with the District Maintenance Manager serving as Chair and the Personnel Assistant serving as Secretary. Appointments to the Committee are to be made by the Chair with Committee approval.

8. Safety Committee members are to be appointed for one-year terms, with two members being replaced from their respective groups every three months. Each initial member shall serve for a minimum of one year. The schedule of change shall be as follows:

First quarter:	Central Division Maintenance, Office Personnel
Second quarter:	Southern Division Maintenance, Planning & Engineering
Third quarter:	Northern Division Maintenance, Naturalists
Fourth quarter:	Rangers, Program Staff

9. Any six members shall constitute a quorum.

10. Minutes of each meeting are to be distributed to all committee members. Corrections may be submitted and will be reviewed by the Secretary and Chair prior to posting. Minutes should be posted at all work locations two weeks after the previous meeting date and copies forwarded to Hennepin Parks risk management consultants.

APPENDIX B

WAIVERS, RELEASES, AGREEMENTS TO PARTICIPATE

WAIVER

Name _____

Address _____

Phone _____

BRYAN POOL WATER SLIDE

BLOOMINGTON / MONROE COUNTY PARK & RECREATION DEPARTMENT

349 S. Walnut
Bloomington, Indiana 47401
332-9668

WAIVER OF CITY LIABILITY

I recognize that because of the potentially hazardous nature of this activity that an injury might be sustained. In the event of such an injury to myself or my child and I or my spouse cannot be contacted, I give permission to the attending physician to render such treatment as would be normal and agree to pay the usual charges for such treatment. I now release the City of Bloomington, the Bloomington/Monroe County Parks and Recreation Department, its employees, agents and assigns for any personal injuries or damages to property caused by or having any relation to this activity. I understand that this release applies to any present or future injuries and that it binds my heirs, executors, and administrators.

I have read this release and understand all of its terms. I sign it voluntarily and with full knowledge of its significance.

_____   _____

Signature   Date

CITY OF KETTERING

PARKS AND RECREATION DIVISION

WAIVER

TO WHOM IT MAY CONCERN:

This is to acknowledge that we, the undersigned, parents or legal guardians of _____ have given the child permission to accompany the Recreation Division excursion to_____ on _____ 19____, by whatever means of transportation the Department deems appropriate.

In consideration of the Department's arranging this excursion and providing transportation for the child, I hereby release and dis- charge the City of Kettering from every claim, liability or demand of any kind for or on account of any personal injury or damage of any kind sustained by the child, whether caused by the negligence of City of Kettering employees or otherwise.

_____   _____
            Date   Parent and/or Guardian

                                          _____
                                              Parent and/or Guardian

(To be signed by both parents or persons having legal custody of the child.)

CITY OF CLEVELAND, DIVISION OF RECREATION

HOLD HARMLESS AGREEMENT
(Trips, Special Events, Participation)

I, the undersigned participant, <u>on behalf of myself, my heirs, legatees, and assigns,</u> hereby agree to indemnify, save, and hold harmless the City of Cleveland or any of their agents, representatives, <u>employees, or assigns,</u> for my health, safety, or any injury <u>and/or disability arising out or</u> resulting from_____.

I have prepared myself for the trip/event/activity in which I am participating <u>by adequately conditioning myself</u> and practicing. I hereby represent that I have no physical restrictions which would prohibit my participation in the trip/event/activity that I have selected. The city of Cleveland has my permission to have a physician attend me if deemed necessary during my trip/event/activity.

<u>I have read and understand the foregoing.</u>

PERTINENT MEDICAL INFORMATION (Special, medications, allergies, other)
PLEASE LIST:

<u>EMERGENCY CONTACTS:</u>

Name _____ Relationship _____ Phone_____

Name _____ Relationship _____ Phone_____

_____
Signature of Participant/Facilities Staff   Date

_____
Signature of Parent/Guardian   Date
(if participant is a minor)

GROUP PARTICIPATION
HOLD HARMLESS AGREEMENT

Most (name of your department) experiences take place outdoors, in conditions often quite different from the controlled environments and predictability of buildings and cities. Nature and weather occur on their own schedule, sometimes unexpectedly, often beyond the control of people to change them.

It is necessary and appropriate in the outdoors for each of us to take responsibilty for taking care of ourselves instead of expecting to be taken care of. We must be aware at all times of where we are, the natural conditions around us and what changes the weather might bring. This need to accept natural features and occurrences on THEIR terms - not necessarily on OURS - is an inevitable and, at the same time, the most wonderful part of the outdoors - its reality, its beauty, and its challenge to us as travelers in the environment.

THE AUTHORIZED GROUP REPRESENTATIVE ON BEHALF OF GROUP MEMBERS AGREES TO PROTECT, INDEMNITY, DEFEND, SAVE AND HOLD HARMLESS THE (NAME OF YOUR DEPARTMENT)ANT ITS OFFICERS AND EMPLOYEES FROM ANY AND ALL CLAIMS, LIABILITIES, DAMAGES OR RIGHT OF ACTION DIRECTLY OR INDIRECTLY ARISING OUT OF THE USE OF (NAME OF YOUR DEPARTMENT) FACILITIES, EQUIPMENT AND/OR PARTICIPATION IN (NAME OF YOUR DEPARTMENT) SPONSORED ACTIVITIES.

Group Name: _____

Activity(s) _____ Park(s) _____

_____ _____

Authorized Group Representative: _____

Address: _____

_____

Phone: _____(W) _____(H)

Signed: _____ _____
  Authorized Representative signing   Date
       on behalf of Permittee

Hold Harmless Agreement Authorized: _____ to _____
                                      date from   date to

WOODSTOCK CHALLENGE ROAD RUN

2 Mile Fun Run   10K Road Race   13K RollerSki Rallye

Registration Information:

1) Make checks payable to the CITY of WOODSTOCK.
2) Please print clearly and supply all information requested.
3) Entries will be processed on an "as-received" basis.
4) Entries received (no postmarks) by September 12 will be confirmed by post-card.
5) **Mailed registration closes September 12.**
6) Course maps available at Woodstock City Hall or by sending a self-addressed, stamped envelope to:
   Woodstock Recreation - Road Run, P.O. Box 190, Woodstock, IL 60098
7) Questions? Call Woodstock Recreation: 815/338-4363. (Staffed Mon-Fri, 9-5; Rec-Line Message thereafter).

OFFICIAL ENTRY FORM

Name _____

Address _____

City _____ State _____ Zip _____

Office Phone ___/_____ Home Phone ___/_____

T-SHIRT SIZE (check one):

CHILD	ADULT
____ 6 - 8	____ Small
____ 10 - 12	____ Medium
____ 14 - 16	____ Large
	____ X-Large

Fun Run _____

10K Race _____

RollerSki _____

RollerBlade _____

Age (as of 9/21) _____

Male _____

Female _____

AMOUNT ENCLOSED $ _____
($1.00 additional for more than one (1) event).

Make Checks Payable To: CITY of WOODSTOCK
Deliver in person: Woodstock City Hall - 121 W. Calhoun
Mail to: Woodstock Recreation - Road Run
   P.O. Box 190
   Woodstock, IL. 60098

ASSUMPTION OF RISK STATEMENT / SIGNATURE SECTION:

On behalf of myself, my heirs, executors, administrators, and assigns, I hereby waive any and all rights and claims for damages I may have against the following sponsors: City of Woodstock, Memorial Hospital for McHenry County, Northwest Newspapers, B. F. Shaw Printing Co., Amcore Bank, and the Banana Belt Cross Country Ski Racing Club, Inc., their heirs, executors, administrators, successors and assigns for any and all injuries which I may suffer while taking part in the Challenge Road Run or as a result thereof.

I also certify that I recognize the difficulties involved with running and rollerskiing/rollerblading, I am sufficiently physically fit to participate, and have not been advised otherwise by a physician.

Moreover, I am aware that there is a degree of risk inherent to these events and that NO MEDICAL INSURANCE IS PROVIDED by any of the sponsors of the Challenge Road Run listed above, nor their staff, employees, members, heirs, executors, successors, assigns or administrators.

SIGNATURE _____ DATED _____

(If under 18, parent or guardian must sign.)

If you do not acknowledge or agree with any part of the conditions listed above, DO NOT PARTICIPATE, nor REGISTER FOR THE CHALLENGE ROAD RUN or BANANABEINER

Does Applicant:

	Have any learning disability	Yes _____	No _____
	Any speech difficulty	Yes _____	No _____
	Any hearing difficulty	Yes _____	No _____

Does Applicant:

	Toilet by self	Yes _____	No _____
	Have bladder control	Yes _____	No _____
	Have bowel control	Yes _____	No _____
	Special needs	Yes _____	No _____

If yes, such as _____

_____

Session enrolling for _____

Additional Comments _____

_____

Other Activities Applicant Is Interested In _____

_____

READ CAREFULLY:

I hereby give my approval to participate in the Bloomington/Monroe County Parks and Recreation Department activity programs for special populations. I do further release, absolve, indemnify and hold harmless the Division of Parks and Recreation, its representatives and supervisors, any and all of them. In case of injury at the site or in transit to or from the site, I hereby waive all claims against the organizers, the sponsors or any of the supervisors appointed to the program. I do further give my permission for the participant to be photographed for possible releases to the media.

DATE _____ _SIGNATURE_ _____

(Must be approved by parent or

guardian)

This application must be filled out and turned in before applicant can participate in program.

PROGRAM FOR SPECIAL POPULATIONS

Return to: Special Populations Coordinator
Parks and Recreation Department
349 South Walnut Street
Bloomington, IN 47401
Phone: 332-9668

Today's Date _____

Name _____

Home Address _____ *Zip* _____ *Phone* _____

Date of Birth _____ *Age* _____ *Sex* _____ *Height* _____ *Weight* _____

School Attending _____ *Teacher* _____

Employment _____

Name of Parent or Guardian _____ *Bus. Phone* _____

In Case of Emergency Contact _____ *Phone* _____

Applicant's Physician _____ *Phone* _____

What disability does applicant have? (Such as retardation, physical handicaps, blind, deaf, emotional, etc.) PLEASE EXPLAIN.

_____

_____

Subject to Seizures? _____

Special instruction relative to seizures _____

_____

Is applicant taking medication at present time? Yes _____ *No* _____

Explain _____

Is applicant allergic to any medication or food? What type? _____

_____

Does Applicant: Use Wheelchair	Yes _____	No _____
Use Crutches	Yes _____	No _____
Use or Wear Braces	Yes _____	No _____
Climb Stairs	Yes _____	No _____
Dress and Undress Self	Yes _____	No _____

COUNTY _____ AREA _____
SCHOOL _____
COACH _____

Indiana Special Olympics
Medical/Press Release

PARENT OR GUARDIAN RELEASE:

☐ Male   ☐ Female

Name _____

Athlete's Address _____

Athlete's City _____ Zip _____

Athlete's Birthdate _____ Age _____

Athlete's Area Code/Phone ____ _____

EMERGENCY INFORMATION
Area Code/Phone of Parent or Guardian

Day ____ _____ Night _____

Name _____

Address _____

City _____ Zip _____

Parent/Guardian or Child's Blue Cross or Other Health Insurance No. _____

If above person cannot be reached, call person below.

Name _____ Area Code/Phone
____ _____

PARENT/GUARDIAN RELEASE:

I, the undersigned parent and/or legal guardian of the above named applicant (hereinafter referred to as the "Entrant"), hereby grant permission for the Entrant to participate in the Special Olympics Program, and on my own and the Entrant's behalf make the following representations, covenants and releases:

It is understood and agreed that Entrant will be participating in the events and using the facilities at his own risk, and with that knowledge the agents, employees and sponsors of the Indiana Special Olympics, and all persons acting in connection therewith are hereby released and discharged from any claim (and it is covenated that no suit will be brought) on behalf of Entrant based on injury, illness or damage to person or property incurred during the course of participation by Entrant in any program of the Indiana Special Olympics, including transportation to and from events, while at any housing facility provided and at the place such event is being held, although not on the field of play or while on the field of play but not participating, and when actually participating in such events.

In permitting the Entrant to participate, I am specifically granting permission to use the likeness, voice and words of the Entrant in television, radio, films, and printed media, for the purpose of advertising or communicating the purposes and activities of Special Olympics and in appealing for funds to support such activities.

As evidence of physical and mental ability to participate in Special Olympics, I submit herewith an executed medical certificate. If I am not present at Special Olympics activities in which the Entrant is to compete, you are authorized on my behalf and at my account to provide such medical and hospital treatment as may be deemed necessary for the health and well-being of the Entrant.

As the parent or guardian of the Entrant, a minor, I authorize Indiana State University Student Health Center, its doctors and nurses, to treat and/or prescribe medications to the above named minor while enrolled or participating in any activity under the auspices of Indiana State University.

Parent/Guardian Signature _____ Dated _____

HEALTH HISTORY: To be filled out by Parent/Guardian or person giving examination

NOTE TO PARENTS: This portion of the form should be filled out carefully by parent or guardian before taking child for his medical examination. The following health information is requested to give the examining physician a basis for his examination:

Significant Illness/Operations: _____

Seizures: Yes ☐ No ☐ Type _____ Medication _____

Allergies: Yes ☐ No ☐ Type _____ Medication _____

Any reaction to penicillin or other drugs ____ If so, what _____

Immunization: ☐ Oral Polio ☐ Measles ☐ Tetanus Toxoid   Date: _____

Other Medication Required by Participant

Type _____ Dosage _____ Time Taken _____

MEDICAL CERTIFICATION: To be completed by Physician, RN, or Paramedic

I have examined the above Entrant to the best of my ability and knowledge, and in my opinion there is no mental or physical reason why he or she should not compete in the Special Olympic Program. Further information will be forwarded, if required. Special medication, if any, is specified on this application.

Physician's, Nurse's or Paramedic's Signature _____ Date _____

COUNCIL • MANAGER • GOVERNMENT

CITY OF
WORTHINGTON
FOUNDED IN 1803

Department of
Parks and Recreation

Participation Agreement
(*MUST BE SIGNED*)

I understand that the Senior Citizen Travel Program has certain risks and hazards inherent with the mode of travel and the places to which I will travel. These risks include but are not limited to: motion sickness, tripping on curbs, steps, stairways, ramps, food borne illness, and motor vehicle accidents.

I also understand and agree to follow the instructions given by the trip coordinator and agree to follow all the rules and regulations of the bus company, the places of sleeping accommodations and the activity director of the site, and the rules and regulations of Worthington   Parks and Recreation as they apply.

I indicate by my signature that I am physically capable of participating in this activity.

Signed_____   Date_____

(*This agreement must be signed before participation in the travel program is allowed.*)

Name_____ Phone_____

Address_____ City_____

In case of emergency, call:_____

  Address_____ Phone_____

My physician is:_____

  Address_____ Phone_____

Physical disabilities:_____

_____

Special dietary requirements:_____

_____

You must provide and carry your own medications. However, you should let the trip director know about them.

SENIOR TRAVEL MEDICAL INFORMATION

FOURTH ANNUAL
SENIOR MASTERS
SPORTS FESTIVAL

LIABILITY WAIVER (MUST BE SIGNED)

In consideration of the right to participate in the 1986 Northwest Open Senior Masters Sports Festival, I do hereby for myself, my heirs, executors, administrators, release and forever discharge any and all claims for damages and losses suffered by me as a result of my participation in or traveling to or from the said events to be held on July 18-27, 1986, or which may hereafter occur to me as a result of my participation, against the Eugene Senior Sports Group, Inc., the sanctioning bodies, the City of Eugene, the University of Oregon, Firs Bowl, Courtsports II Fitness Center, Lane Community College, Fiddlers' Green Golf Course, Shadow Hills Golf Course, Willow Creek Racquet Club, Oregon Track Club, Bethel School District, The Bon, Bi-Mart, and/or any officers or agents thereof.

I further understand that there are certain risks and that accidents and/or injuries may occur in the various sports and that certain sports require proper training and proper physical conditioning. Knowing the risks and conditions required for my sport, nevertheless, I hereby agree to assume those risks and release and hold harmless all those persons or entities mentioned above.

I grant to the Eugene Senior Sports Group, Inc. the right to use any pictures taken of me during the Senior Masters Sports Group, Inc. the right to use any pictures taken of me during the Senior Masters Sports Festival to be held July 18 through July 27, 1986 without my remuneration.

I certify that I have read and understand the above.

Participant's signature _____

Date _____

CITY OF KETTERING
PARKS AND RECREATION DIVISION
ROSE E. MILLER RECREATION CENTER
3201 Marshall Road
Kettering, Ohio 45429

PHYSICIAN'S TRIP RELEASE FORM

Being the physician of _____, I hereby acknowledge that he/she is physically able to participate in the City of Kettering Parks and Recreation Division's Senior Citizen Club's trip to _____ from _____.

_____
Physician's Name

_____
Date

INDEMNIFICATION AGREEMENT AND RELEASE FROM LIABILITY

I, _____, enter this indemnification agreement
and release from liability on behalf of the _____,
sponsor of _____ softball team, which has organized
a softball tournament to be held on City of Eugene property. At this
tournament, said sponsor intends to dispense alcoholic beverages through
team members and others. I acknowledge that there are some dangers associated
with the use and misuse of alcohol, both for the consumer and third parties.

I agree to indemnify, hold harmless and defend the City of Eugene, its
officials, agents and employees from and against any and all claims,
damages, losses and expenses including attorneys fees arising from any
occurence causing damage or injury to any party participating in said
tournament or any third parties injured during or as a result of this event.
I further agree to repair or reimburse the City for any and all damages to
City property caused directly or indirectly by this activity.

I have read the preceeding and understand that this is a release of
liability and a contract between myself, on behalf of the sponsor, and the
City of Eugene and its employees and agents. I am signing this release of my
own free will and have authority to so bind the sponsor.

Signed: Dated:

_____   _____

81

22807 Woods Chapel Road
Blue Springs, Missouri 640
(816) 795-8200

TEAM ROSTER & PARTICIPATION AGREEMENT

TEAM NAME: _____ LEAGUE: _____ DIVISION: _____

LOCATION: _____ DAY: _____

TEAM MANAGER: _____ PHONE: _____

ADDRESS: _____ CITY: _____ STATE: _____ ZIP: _____
                                          Day   Night

In consideration for being allowed to participate in this league, we the undersigned, hereby waive all claims for injury or accident or liability of any kind and do hereby release the Jackson County Parks and Recreation Department, its staff, all managers, sponsors, director officials or owners of the property on which the facility is located, from any claims, now or in the future, for such injury or accident.

	PLAYER'S SIGNATURE	STREET, CITY, STATE, ZIP	PHONE: WORK # ON
1.			
2.			
3.			
4.			
5.			
6.			
7.			
8.			
9.			
10.			
11.			
12.			
13.			
14.			
15.			
16.			
17.			
18.			

As the manager of a recreational sport team, I accept a position of responsibility as an intermediary between the recreation staff and the members of my team. I also accept full responsibility for the conduct of my team players and all affairs regarding my team. As manager I will promote good sportsmanship among all players, win or lose.

MANAGER'S SIGNATURE: _____

CITY OF KETTERING
PARKS AND RECREATION DIVISION
PLAYER'S CONTRACT

TEAM: ☐☐☐☐☐☐☐☐☐☐☐☐☐ SPORT: ☐☐☐☐☐☐☐☐☐☐☐ CLASS: ☐

(Please type or print)

DAY OF WEEK: ☐☐☐☐☐☐ LOCATION: ☐☐☐☐☐☐ MANAGER: ☐☐☐☐☐☐☐☐☐☐☐☐☐☐

NAME: ☐☐☐☐☐☐☐☐☐☐☐☐☐ ☐☐☐☐☐☐☐☐☐☐☐ PHONE: ☐☐☐ ☐☐☐☐

(Last name) (First name) (Area) (Phone)

ADDRESS: ☐☐☐☐☐☐☐☐☐☐☐☐☐☐☐ ☐☐☐☐☐☐☐☐☐☐☐☐☐ ☐☐☐☐☐

(Street) (City) (Zip)

DO YOU LIVE IN KETTERING? ☐ ☐   DO YOU WORK IN KETTERING? ☐ ☐ IF YES, ☐☐☐☐☐☐☐☐☐☐☐☐☐☐☐☐

yes no   yes no   (Employer)

PRESENT AGE: ☐☐   DATE OF BIRTH: ☐☐ ☐☐ ☐☐   DOCTOR'S NAME: ☐☐☐☐☐☐☐☐☐☐☐☐☐☐☐☐

Month Day Year

I, THE UNDERSIGNED, hereby agree to play with the above team during the playing season of 19___, or until I am given my release in writing by said team and said is recorded in the office of the City of Kettering Parks and Recreation Division. I promise to observe and abide by the rules and regulations of the Kettering Parks and Recreation Division and the league to which the above team is a member. I release the City of Kettering Parks and Recreation Division of any financial responsibilities due to injuries received while playing, practicing or traveling with above-mentioned team during the current season. I am in good health and do not have any physical reason why I cannot play this sport.

_____

(Player's Signature)

DATE SIGNED: ☐☐ ☐☐ ☐☐

Month Day Year

DATE FILED: ☐☐ ☐☐ ☐☐

Month Day Year

NOTE: THIS FORM MUST BE FILLED OUT BEFORE
YOU WILL BE PERMITTED TO PARTICIPATE

DEPARTMENT OF PARKS AND RECREATION

(Parent's Permission Certificate)

I would like for _____, my son or
           (First)   (Initial)   (Last)

daughter to participate in a trip/program sponsored by the Department

of Parks and Recreation to/at _____
                                  (Event)

_____ on _____.
      (Place)   (Date)

I understand that the Department of Parks and Recreation cannot be

held responsible in the event of accident or injury to a participant.

I hereby give my consent.

_____   _____
      (Date)   (Parent or Guardian)

Cuyahoga Falls
Park & Recreation Dept.   DATE_____

I hereby grant permission to my child_____

_____to go on a_____

to_____on_____

under the supervision of_____
I release the City of Cuyahoga Falls and its representatives
from all liabilities from any and all injuries sustained by
my child during the above

_____.

                Signed_____
                    Parent or Guardian

Redmond Parks & Recreation Registration Form

15670 NE 85th St., Redmond WA 98052, 882-6401
(Only one family per form. Photocopies are accepted.)

NAME

Adult Last name:_____First_____

Adult Last name: _____First: _____

Child _____Age_____Child _____Age_____

* Day phone _____ * Evening Phone _____

*Mailing Address _____City_____Zip_____

Work address (if applicable)_____City_____Zip_____

* ☐ Check if this is a new address or phone #.

Participant Name	Program Number	Program Name	Fee	Program Number of Acceptable Alternative

WAIVER OF LIABILITY   **TOTAL $** _____

ALL participants are requested to sign the following release. Parents or guardians must sign for minors. I/We assume all risks and hazards incidental to such participation including transportation to and from the activities and do hereby waive, release, absolve, indemnify and agree to hold harmless City of Redmond Parks and Recreation Department, park supervisors, instructors and persons transporting myself or my/our child for any claim arising out of any injury to myself or my/our child.

Signature(s) _____ Date_____

Help us to serve you better

I/we live in:

☐ 1 Redmond City Limits
☐ 2 Unincorporated King County
☐ 3 Other City

ACTIVITY REGISTRATION FORM

PLEASE PRINT & FILL OUT COMPLETELY

ADULT NAME	LAST													FIRST										MI		ADULT IDENTIFICATION #							
	ADDRESS																										DEMOGRAPHIC AREA						
	CITY											STATE			ZIP CODE								COMMENT										
PHONE NO.'s	(DAY)				—			(NIGHT)			—				(EMERG.)			—			REDUCED FEE APPLICATION #										

PARTICIPANT NAME				AGE	SEX	MEDICAL ALERT	ACTIVITY NO.s		ACTIVITY NAME (1st Choice)	MISC.		ACTIVITY FEE	NON-RES. FEE	TOTAL FEES
LAST		FIRST	MI				1st Choice	2nd Choice		DISC.	FEE			

TOTAL FEES $

REFUNDS

Activities are either offered or cancelled based on the enrollment since the fees collected must offset personnel, equipment, and other program expenses. Sufficient time is also necessary to notify registrants when a program must be cancelled. Therefore, any requests for a refund must be made at least 72 hours prior to the scheduled starting session- requests after this time will **not** be considered. We cannot be responsible for circumstances beyond our control. There will be a $3 service charge for each activity refund processed.
   In the event that an activity is filled, cancelled or a schedule change prohibits participation, a full refund will be made. Please allow up to 4 weeks for refunds to be issued.

WAIVER

In consideration of your accepting mine or my child's entry, I hereby for myself, my child, my heirs, my executors, and administrators, waive and release any and all rights and claims for damages I or my child might have against the City of Billings and/or School District No. 2 and its representatives, successors and assigns for any and all injuries suffered by myself or my child at any activity sponsored by these groups.

FORM OF PAYMENT

☐ 1 CASH
☐ 2 CHECK #_____
☐ 3 MONEY ORDER

DEPARTMENT OF PARKS, RECREATION & PUBLIC LANDS
P.O. BOX 1178
510 NORTH BROADWAY
BILLINGS, MONTANA 59103
(406) 657-8371

DATE_____

Signature of Parent
Guardian_____

(PLEASE READ INFORMATION ON REVERSE SIDE)

Make check(s) or money orders payable to:

CITY OF BILLINGS

AMOUNT ENCL. $

REGISTRATION FORM

Please return completed form along with proper fee to: Bensenville Park District, 161 North Church Road, Bensenville, Illinois 60106 (312) 766-7015.

Family Last Name _____ Family Registration # _____

Address _____ City _____ Zip _____

Home Phone _____ Work/Emergency Phone _____

FIRST NAME	AGE	CHOICE	PROGRAM	PROGRAM NUMBER	DAY	DATE	TIME	FEE
		1st						
		2nd						
		1st						
		2nd						
		1st						
		2nd						
		1st						
		2nd						
		1st						
		2nd						
		1st						
		2nd						

"As a participant in the program, I recognize and acknowledge that there are certain risks of physical injury and I agree to assume the full risk of any injuries, including loss of life, damages or loss which I may sustain as a result of participating in any and all activities connected with or associated with such program."

I further agree to waive and relinquish all claims, fully release and discharge and agree to indemnify and hold harmless and defend the park district and its officers, agents, servants and employees from any and all claims resulting from injuries, including loss of life, damages and losses sustained by me and arising out of, connected with, or in any way associated with the activities of the program.

Participants signature _____

Parent or Guardian Signature _____
(for participants 17 years and under)

NOTE: This registration form cannot be processed without the above signature.
        Thank you for your cooperation.

PROGRAM PARTICIPANT AGREEMENTS (GROUPS)

RELEASE DATE: October 30, 1986
REPLACES ISSUE DATED:

DEPARTMENT RESPONSIBLE: Management Services/Operations

Policy

The (name of your department) requires that "group participant" and "hold harmless" agreements be signed by an authorized group representative on behalf of individual group members participating in outdoor skills/training programs and competitive events or other program activity of potential risk conducted by Park District staff, volunteers, co-sponsor, or Park District contractors.

Representative examples of applicable programs include, but are not limited to, downhill skiing, cross-country skiing and golf lessons; canoeing, sailing and other water-related skills programs; challenge hikes, fun runs and triathlons; day trips, overnight camping and field trips, where park users are required to actively participate and are under the supervision of a Park Distrcit employee, volunteer, co-sponsor or Park District contractor.

Non-participatory presentations and demonstrations are explicitly excluded from this policy. However, program leaders must present verbal declaration of potential risks and safety precautions to all participants.

General Information

Group participant agreements are statements of fact disclosing the roles and responsibilities of the Park District and group leaders relating to participants. Accordingly, agreements should be drafted to reflect the specific circumstances of a particular program and include the following components:

o Recognition of the nature of the activity potential risks inherent in the activity and/or participation with others.

o Reference specific rules and regulations and acknowledge by the agreement that the participant will obey these rules and regulations, the person in charge and assist in informing/calling attention to situations that may cause injury.

o Acknowledgement of the fitness requirements that group members should possess to participate in the activity.

Sample group participant agreements are available and on file in the office of the Director of the Department of Management Services.

In addition to group participant agreements group representatives are to execute a hold harmless agreement.

The Hold Harmless agreement states that THE GROUP REPRESENTATIVE ON BEHALF OF GROUP MEMBERS AGREES TO PROTECT, INDEMNIFY, DEFEND, SAVE AND HOLD HARMLESS THE (NAME OF YOUR DEPARTMENT) AND ITS OFFICERS AND EMPLOYEES FROM ANY AND ALL CLAIMS, LIABILITIES, DAMAGES OR RIGHT OF ACTION DIRECTLY OR INDIRECTLY ARISING OUT OF THE USE OF (NAME OF YOUR DEPARTMENT) AREAS, FACILITIES, EQUIPMENT AND/OR PARTICIPATION IN A (NAME OF YOUR DEPARTMENT) SPONSORED ACTIVITY.

Procedures

Group participant agreements are to be prepared by the Division Recreation Supervisor, Outdoor Education Supervisor, or Special Facility Manager, responsible for a given program. In those instances where programs are offered on a District-wide basis (e.g., cross-country ski lessons) a common participant agreement will be used for groups at all locations. Upon request the Director of Management Services and the Park District's Risk Manager will assist supervisors in formulating the participant agreements.

A signed and dated copy of the group participant agreement must be obtained from group leaders prior to their group participation.

The Group Hold Harmless Agreement Form is to be sent to the group by the appropriate (name of your department) supervisor. Agreements must be completed, signed, dated and returned to the supervisor prior to group participation. Signed copies are to be sent to and kept on file in the office of the Director of Management Services.

In cases where a group, such as a school or community agency, is a regular participant in Park District programs only one Group Hold Harmless Agreement need be on file for that group. The Agreement will remain valid for one year at which time a new agreement must be executed.

Copies of the signed and dated agreements are to be retained by the supervisor with a single sample copy of the group participant agreements forwarded to the Director of Management Services. Copies of the agreements are to be retained by supervisors for 12 months after the date of agreement. They may be disposed of thereafter provided no notice of claim has been filed or received and there is no reason to believe that such a claim is forthcoming.

PROGRAM PARTICIPANT AGREEMENTS (INDIVIDUALS)

RELEASE DATE: October 30, 19
REPLACES ISSUE DATED:

DEPARTMENT RESPONSIBLE: Management Services/Operations

Policy:

The Suburban Hennepin Regional Park District requires that participant agreements be signed by all persons (parent or legal guardian in the case of minors under 18 years of age) participating in outdoor skills/training programs and competitive events or other program activity of potential risk conducted by Park District staff, volunteers, co-sponsor, or Park District contractors. Representative examples of applicable programs include, but are not limited to, downhill skiing, cross-country skiing and golf lessons; canoeing, sailing and other water-related skills programs; challenge hikes, fun runs and triathalons; day trips, overnight camping and field trips, where park users are required to actively participate and are under the supervision of a Park District employee, volunteer, co-sponsor or Park District contractor. Non-participatory presentations and demonstrations are explicity excluded from this policy. However, minimally in all instances, a verbal declaration of potential risks and safety precautions should be presented to all participants.

General Information

Participant agreements are statements of fact disclosing the roles and responsibilities of the Park District and participants. Accordingly, agreements should be drafted to reflect the specific circumstances of a particular program and include the following components:

o Recognition of the nature of the activity potential risks inherent in the activity and/or participation with others.

91

o Reference specific rules and regulations and acknowledge by the agreement that the participant will obey these rules and regulations, the person in charge and assist in informing/calling attention to situations that may cause injury.

o Acknowledgment that the participant is physically fit to participate in the activity.

Sample participant agreements are available and on file in the office of the Director of the Department of Management Services.

Procedures

Participant agreements are to be prepared by the Division Recreation Supervisor, Outdoor Education Supervisor, or Special Facility Manager, responsible for a given program. In those instances where programs are offered on a District-wide basis (e.g., cross-country ski lessons) a common participant agreement will be used for participants at all locations. Upon request the Director of Management Services and the Park District's Risk Manager will assist supervisors in formulating the participant agreements.

A signed and dated copy of the participant agreement must be obtained from all program participants prior to their participation. In the case of minors under 18 years of age signatures must be obtained form the parent or legal guardian with specific reference to the minor who is participating in the program.

Copies of the signed and dated agreements are to be retained by the supervisor with a single sample copy of the agreement form specifically referencing the program location and date forwarded to the Director of Management Services. Copies of the signed agreements are to be retained by supervisors for 12 months after the program. They may be disposed of thereafter provided no notice of claim has been filed or received and there is no reason to believe that such a claim is forthcoming.

SUBURBAN HENNEPIN REGIONAL PARK DISTRICT

Participant Agreement

PROGRAM   LOCATION:
Winter Camping

Most Hennepin Parks experiences take place outdoors, in conditions often quite different from the controlled environments and predictability of buildings and cities. Nature and weather occur on their own schedule, sometimes unexpectedly, often beyond the control of people to change them.

It is necessary and appropriate in the outdoors for each of us to take responsibility for taking care of ourselves instead of expecting to be taken care of. We must be aware at all times of where we are, the natural conditions around us and what changes the weather might bring. This need to accept natural features and occurrences on THEIR terms - not necessarily on OURS - is an inevitable and, at the same time, the most wonderful part of the outdoors - it's reality, it's beauty, and it's challenge to us as travellers in the environment.

The undersigned, accepted as a participant in the winter camping program offered by the Suburban Hennepin Regional Park District, agrees as follows:

1. I acknowledge that winter camping requires strenuous physical activity and endurance.

2. I fully understand that winter temperature, winds and occasional storms can be a factor in the winter camping experience. I further realize that there are elements of physical risk such as frost nip, frost bite, hypothermia and other winter-related conditions.

3. I understand that there are many unpredictable, changing conditions potentially affecting the winter camping environment and experience such as conditions of trails, camping sites, wildlife behavior and other natural occurances.

4. I certify that, to the best of my knowledge, I have no physical, mental or emotional condition which might be aggravated by this activity, which might in any way inconvenience or endanger staff or other participants, or which might impair my ability to participate in and withstand all possible winter camping activities.

5. I will obey all rules, regulations and directives of the Suburban
    Hennepin Regional Park District and of the person in charge, and
    will assist by informing and/or calling to the attention of the
    person in charge any situation which might result in injury.

Thus acknowledging the rigors of all activities connected with winter camping
and the unpredictability and power of natural and weather events, and in
consideration for being accepted as a participant in the winter camping
program, I hereby accept all responsibility for taking care of myself and for
any damage to my equipment or injuries to myself while participating in the
above designated program. I agree, therefore, that the Suburban Hennepin
Regional Park District, their agents and employees, will not be liable for any
damages or injuries directly or approximately caused by any act, happening or
event.

DATE: _____   _____
                                    Signature of Participant

I (we) parent(s) of [or legal guardian(s)] for _____
hereby consent to her/him participating in above designated program and have
signed the above participant agreement on behalf of said minor.

Signed _____   Date _____

<u>SUBURBAN HENNEPIN REGIONAL PARK DISTRICT</u>

Participant Agreement

<u>PROGRAM</u>:   <u>LOCATION</u>:
Cross-Country Skiing

Most Hennepin Parks experiences take place outdoors, in conditions often quite different from the controlled environments and predictability of buildings and cities. Nature and weather occur on their own schedule, sometimes unexpectedly, often beyond the control of people to change them.

It is necessary and appropriate in the outdoors for each of us to take responsibility for taking care of ourselves instead of expecting to be taken care of. We must be aware at all times of where we are, the natural conditions around us and what changes the weather might bring. This need to accept natural features and occurrences on THEIR terms - not necessarily on OURS - is an inevitable and, at the same time, the most wonderful part of the outdoors - its reality, its beauty, and its challenge to us as travellers in the environment.

The undersigned, a participant in the cross-country skiing program, offered by the Suburban Hennepin Regional Park District agrees as follows:

1. I acknowledge that cross-country skiing requires strenuous physical activity and endurance.

2. Trail conditions, weather, and other people affect the overall cross-country skiing experience. I am aware of the factors that follows:

   - The program may take place on trails that are groomed or ungroomed. The terrain of these trails varies greatly and trail conditions may be icy or rough, depending on weather and other skiers.

   - Winds, temperature, and occasional storms can affect the cross-country skiing experience. I realize that I should take precautions and guard for frost-bite, hypothermia, frost nip, and other winter-related conditions.

   - I understand that I should be aware of other skiers at all times in order to avoid possible collison.

95

3. I certify that, to the best of my knowledge, I have no physical,mental or emotional condition which might be aggravated by this activity, which might in any way inconvenience or endanger staff or other participants, or which might impair my ability to participate in and withstand all possible cross-country skiing activities.

4. I will obey all rules, regulations and directives of the Suburban Hennepin Regional Park District and of the person in charge, and will assist by informing and/or calling to the attention of the person in charge any situation which might result in injury.

Thus acknowledging the rigors of all activities connected with cross-country skiing and the unpredictability and power of natural and weather events, and in consideration for being accepted as a participant in the winter camping program, I hereby accept all responsibility for taking care of myself and for any damage to my equipment or injuries to myself while participating in the above designated program. I agree, therefore, that the Suburban Hennepin Regional Park District, their agents and employees, will not be liable for any damages or injuries directly or approximately caused by any act, happening or event.

DATE: _____   _____
                                   Signature or Participant

I (we) parent(s) of [or legal guardian(s)] for _____
hereby consent to her/him participating in above designated program and have signed the above participant agreement on behalf of said minor.

Signed _____   Date _____

CITY OF KETTERING
PARKS AND RECREATION DIVISION
TOT LOT PROGRAM
PERMISSION SLIP

You have my permission for _____ (Child's Name) to participate in all activities that may take him away from the classrooms. These are supervised walks to the park, or to promote and encourage environmental awareness. I understand that I will be notified in advance about any trip that would take my child away from City grounds.

_____
Parent or Guardian Signature

CITY OF KETTERING
PARKS AND RECREATION DIVISION
TOT LOT PROGRAM
PERMISSION SLIP

You have my permission to take _____ (Child's Name) picture for newspaper purposes.

_____
Parent or Guardian Signature

EQUIPMENT AND SUPPLY LOAN AGREEMENT

The undersigned and the City of Kettering, in consideration of the mutual covenants hereinafter expressed, agree as follows:

The City agrees to loan the following described property to the undersigned:

Item	Inventory No.	Condition
_____	_____	_____
_____	_____	_____
_____	_____	_____
_____	_____	_____
_____	_____	_____

Conditions:

1. Acceptance or retention shall constitute acknowledgement that such property was received in good order and repair.

2. The term shall commence _____.
    (date)

3. The term shall terminate _____.
    (date)

4. The property shall at all times remain the sole property of the City and the undersigned shall have no right to the property. The property shall not be transferred or delivered to any other person and returned upon demand.

5. The undersigned agrees to keep and maintain the property with proper care and shall be liable to the City for any loss or damage to the property up to the valuation of the property as listed on the schedule in effect at the time of execution.

    We agree to the above stated regulations and responsibilities.

_____   _____
Organization Name   Date

_____
Signature of Organizational Representative

_____
Address   Phone Number

APPENDIX C

USE PERMITS, INDIGENT AGREEMENTS

GUIDELINES FOR EVENTS PLANNED IN CITY OF EUGENE PARKS AND FACILITIES
DEVELOPED BY: City of Eugene, Parks and Recreation Department
          777 Hight Street, Suite 102, Eugene OR 97401-2750
          Phone: 687-5333

Welcome to Eugene's parks! We're pleased you've decided to take advantage of our attractive parks and facilities for the scheduling of your event. In order for your event to go as smoothly as possible, we've put together this guide-line of requirements to assist your planning.

1: COMPLETE THE "STATEMENT OF INTENDED USE OF CITY PARK" form which can be obtained from the Parks and Recreation Office. Return the completed form to Dave Pompel, Business Manager for the Department at the same office at 777 High Street, Suite 102.
NOTE: Before any promotion of your event is done, this form must be reviewed and approved by the Business Manager.

2: SECURITY MAY BE REQUIRED depending upon the type and anticipated attendance of your event. When reviewing your "Statement of . . " form, our Business Manager will advise if security will be required. If security is necessary, it may be required to take the form of Parks and Recreation Department staff, off-duty City of Eugene Police or be provided by the event organizers. The type and provider of the security will be determined by the City of Eugene's Police and Parks and Recreation Departments.

3: SANITATION AND RESTROOM REQUIREMENTS. The current requirements for toilets are one restroom for each sex for every 200 participants. If there are not sufficient on-site restrooms available, portable restrooms will have to be provided and removed with the City's approval at the organizer's expense.

4: SITE AND FACILITY CLEANUP. The event organizers will be expected to completely clean up the site and facilities used during the event at its conclusion. You will be responsible to arrange with our Parks Services Division (687-5334) for additional garbage containers. If the event will cause excessive garbage, you will be required to provide trash bags and may have to pay to have the garbage removed.

5. FOOD SERVING. If food is served, sold or given away, a "TEMPORARY RESTAURANT LICENSE" must be obtained from the Lane County Health Department (687-3731). The cost of the license runs from $10 to $40. It may also be necessary for you to obtain a "CERTIFICATE OF INSUR-ANCE" naming the City of Eugene as an insured. Our Business Manager will inform you of this requirement if it applies.

6: SERVING BEER OR WINE. WITH APPROVAL from the Parks and Recreation Executive Manager, the serving of beer or wine may be allowed in park areas and facilities dependent upon the location. (Refer to "PARK RULES" available from the Parks and Recreation Department.) Approval is contingent upon successful application of an Oregon Liquor Control Commission (OLCC-686-7739) beer/wine license and observance of all OLCC rules and regulations. An OLCC permit is REQUIRED if you plan to charge or accept money for the beer or wine. The expense of this permit will be the organizer's responsibility.

IF YOU ARE APPROVED TO SERVE BEER AND OR WINE, YOU MUST:
A. Observe and enforce all OLCC rules pertinent to your event,
B. Mark off an area where the beer/wine will be consumed, and
C. Supervise, with responsible adults, the marked off area when it
is in use to make sure that there are no minors drinking and
that no one is drinking too much.

OLCC permit applications can be obtained from the OLCC office at 132 East Broadway, completed by the applicant and taken to the City of Eugene's Permit and Information Center at 244 East Broadway with a $25 application processing fee. Processing takes one week and the form can then be returned to the OLCC office to obtain the permit which costs $10 per day.

7: AMPLIFIED SOUND is permitted ONLY with prior approval from the Business Manager of the Parks and Recreation Department. Amplified music is allowed ONLY in connection with events of general community interest and is limited to two hours per day in a City park.

8: ELECTRICITY. Use of electrical outlets must be approved in advance by the Business Manager. Determining outlet locations and service can be obtained by calling the Parks Service division at 687-5334. An electricity use charge may be necessary and for staff time that may be required to establish power.

9: LIGHTS for softball fields and tennis courts must be approved in advance and a per hour charge imposed for their use as well as any staff time required to operate the lights.

10: ANTICIPATED PARTICIPANTS you list on the "Statement of Intended Use" form will be reviewed by our Business Manager in relation to the size of your requested park or facility. It may be necessary to renegotiate your original request to a park or facility more suitable to the event you have planned.

11: PRIORITY OF EVENTS. Programs, events and activities sponsored by the Parks and Recreation Department will take precedent over outside group requests.

12: VEHICLES IN THE PARKS are prohibited without prior approval from the Parks Services Superintendent, 687-5334. Even with approval, vehicle entry authorization is restricted to limited access areas.

Based on this information, you should have a good idea of what is required for your successful event. If you should need further information, contact our Business Manager David Pompel, at 687-5302 whose office is within the Administrative offices of the Parks and Recreation Department, 777 High Street Suite 260. Additional event planning information is available from the staff at Parks Services division, 210 Cheshire Street, within from Skinner Butte Park.

Revised 9/17/86*radtpuse

Building Use Permit

Independent School District No. 279
(OSSEO AREA SCHOOLS)

COMMUNITY
EDUCATION
& SERVICES

SCHOOL

_____

FACILITY

_____

ACTIVITY WILL BEGIN AT —

_____ END AT _____

GROUP DESIRES TO ENTER BUILDING AT

_____

DAYS DESIRED: M T W TH F S S

DATES

_____

DATES FACILITY IS **NOT** AVAILABLE FOR YOUR GROUP ARE:

SERIES OF MEETINGS

_____

NUMBER ATTENDING

_____

DATE OF APPLICATION

_____

DISTRIBUTION OF FORM:

White	— School Office
Blue	— Custodian
Green	— Building Supervisor
Yellow	— Community Education
Pink	— Business Office
Gold	— Organization

OPTIONAL COPIES:

☐ Cook
☐ Food Service Office
☐ Classroom Teacher
☐ School Media Coordinator

EQUIPMENT NEEDS:

PHY ED

_____

_____

AUDIO /VISUAL

_____

_____

OTHER

_____

_____

_____
Name of Organization

_____
Person Responsible

_____
Street Address

_____
City, State, Zip

BUSINESS PHONE   HOME PHONE

SPECIFIC ACTIVITY

ESTIMATED FEES:

$ _____ . . . . RENTAL

$ _____ . . . . CUSTODIAL

$ _____ . . . . COOK

$ _____ . . . . . . _____

$ _____ . . . . . . _____

NOTICE: Custodial charges may be assessed if **facility is not left in its original condition.**

I.S.D. No. 279 does not discriminate on the basis of sex, religion, economic status, age or marital status in any area of the educational program or personnel practices.

APPROVAL:

_____   _____
BUILDING PRINCIPAL   COMMUNITY EDUCATION COORDINATOR

103

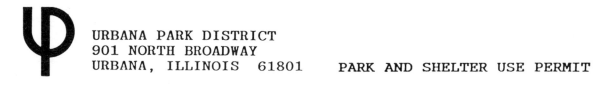

URBANA PARK DISTRICT
901 NORTH BROADWAY
URBANA, ILLINOIS 61801   **PARK AND SHELTER USE PERMIT**

Permission is hereby granted to _____
                                  (Organization)

                                  _____
                                  (Applicant's Name)

                                  _____
                                  (Address)

                                  _____
                                  (Home Phone)   (Work Phone)

To use _____

Date _____   Time _____

Purpose _____

Will Admission be charged? _____ Purpose _____

Approximate number of people _____

Special arrangements _____

                      _____

                      _____

NOTE: Alcoholic beverages are not allowed in Urbana Parks unless
an Alcoholic Beverage Permit has been issued to the organization
and/or applicant.

I have reviewed the Use of Parks and Shelters terms and
conditions (see p.108) and will abide by them.

Signed: Approved:

_____   _____
Applicant   Urbana Park District

_____   _____
Date   Date

                                Rental Fee_____

     White-Public   Pink-Operations   Yellow-Office File

CITY OF MAPLE GROVE
PARKS AND RECREATION BOARD
9401 Fernbrook Lane
Maple Grove, MN 55369

№ 2376

SHELTER BUILDING USE PERMIT

This Permit must be received
ten (10) days prior to event.

DATE OF APPLICATION _____

NAME OF USER _____

PERSON RESPONSIBLE _____ HOME PHONE _____ WORK PHONE _____

ADDRESS _____ ZIP _____

FACILITY REQUESTED _____

PURPOSE OF USE _____

_____

_____

IS KITCHEN TO BE USED? YES ___ NO ___ IF YES, LIST ITEMS AND APPLIANCES TO BE USED. _____

_____

DAY AND DATE REQUESTED _____

HOURS: FROM _____ TO _____

APPROXIMATE NUMBER ATTENDING _____

EQUIPMENT OR FACILITIES REQUESTED _____

SPECIAL PERMISSION IS REQUESTED FOR: _____

_____

DEPOSITS: _____   FEES: _____

_____   _____

_____   _____

_____   _____

_____   _____

_____   _____

TOTAL _____   TOTAL _____

As the official designee of the authorized user I hereby pledge to conform to all the ordinances, regulations and policies established by the Parks and Recreation Board governing the use of all park and recreational facilities and accept full responsibility for any damage done by those I represent.

SIGNED _____

DATE _____

AUTHORIZED BY _____

DATE _____

PLEASE OBSERVE THE PARKS AND RECREATION BOARD REGULATIONS
White - Office   Canary - Organization   Pink - Maintenance

LIABILITY WAIVER AND HOLD HARMLESS AGREEMENT

I, _____, represent that I am a member of the
_____ and have on behalf of
that organization applied for a parks use permit from the City of Eugene.
I acknowledge that the City requires proof of liability insurance prior
to issuing permits for the use of City parks. I have truthfully filed
an affidavit of indigency with the City in connection with the application
for a parks permit. The event for which application is made is scheduled
to be held on _____, 1986 at or about the following places
_____.

I agree and bind my organization to hold the City of Eugene harmless from
any claim for damage or injury arising out of our activities in connection with this event. I understand that this agreement to indemnify
is for any and all liability of the City of Eugene, including costs of
defense and attorney fees arising from any activity on our part which
is legally negligent, reckless or a violation of a legal duty owed by
us to the city of Eugene or any third person. We do not indemnify the
City of Eugene from its own separate negligence in connection with this
event but only from derivative liability arising from our activities
in connection therewith.

I have read this agreement carefully and know and understand its terms.
I agree to supervise the conduct of the event to the best of my abilities
and to the extent feasible and, specifically, to supervise compliance of
the event participants with the permit requirements and other regulations
applicable to the use of City of Eugene parks.

Should any litigation arise from this agreement the prevailing party at
trial and, if taken, any decided appeal, shall be entitled to be awarded
its reasonable attorney fees incurred therein.

Dated this _____ day of _____, 1986.

_____
Applicant

AFFIDAVIT

STATE OF OREGON)
) ss.
County of Lane)

    I, _____, being duly sworn do hereby depose
and say:

    On behalf of _____, I have filed
an application for a parks use permit with the City of Eugene. I state
that on the basis of my personal knowledge that the assets and operating
income of _____ are insufficient at the present
time to pay the premium on a certificate of insurance that may be
required as a condition of granting a parks use permit. I further state
that I have authority from _____, which I
represent, to apply for the parks use permit and to execute this affidavit
of indigency. I further state that the permit application and this affidavit
have been executed by me with the knowledge and consent of the officers
of _____ or those who are in control of that
organization.

    DATED this _____ day of _____, 1986.

                                 _____

    SUBSCRIBED AND SWORN to before me this _____ day of
_____, 1986.

                                 _____
                                 Notary Public for Oregon
                                 My Commission Expires: _____

URBANA PARK DISTRICT
USE OF PARKS AND SHELTERS

1. A Park Use Permit is required for any group of twenty-five (25) or more.

2. Groups, organizations, and individuals using the parks and/or facilities will comply with the laws of the State of Illinois, the City of Urbana, and the Urbana Park District.

3. Alcoholic beverages are not allowed in Urbana Parks unless an Alcoholic Beverage Permit has been issued to the organization and/or applicant.

4. All activities shall be properly controlled and supervised. Whenever persons participating in the planned activity are under 18 years of age, adequate adult chaperones must be provided.

5. No loud or excessive noises will take place that will disturb other users of the park or park neighbors.

6. The Park Board, the Director of Parks and Recreation, other authorized personnel or the City of Urbana Police may revoke any permit previously granted, at any time, if it is determined that the application for permit contained any misrepresentation or false statement, or that any condition set forth in the policies governing the permit requested is not being complied with, or that the safety of the participants in the activities of the applicant or other patrons or visitors to the parks is endangered by the continuation of such activity.

7. No person shall solicit contributions, nor offer to sell or exchange any article or thing, nor buy or offer to buy any article or thing, for any purpose whatsoever, within any of the Parks of the District, except by permission of the Director or Board of Commissioners.

8. Permit holder agrees to deposit all trash and litter (resulting from the event) in trash receptacles.

9. No person shall park any motor vehicle in any of the parks of the District except in areas specifically designated for the parking of such vehicles.

10. The applicant agrees to assume liability for any damage done to any District property.

11. Urbana Park District will not be liable for any claims for injury or damages resulting from or arising out of the use of the District's facility or premises and the permit holder agrees to indemnify the Park District and hold it harmless against any and all such claims, damages, losses and expenses. If requested by the District, the permit holder shall carry insurance against such claims and furnish the District with a certificate of insurance evidencing same.

APPENDIX D

ACCIDENT REPORT FORMS

BENSENVILLE PARK DISTRICT
ACCIDENT/INJURY REPORT

2311

(1) DATE OF ACCIDENT _____ (DAY) (MO) (DAY) (YR) (2) TIME OF ACCIDENT ___:___ ___ M. (3) DATE OF REPORT _____ (DAY) (MO) (DAY) (YR)

(4) AREA: ☐ PARK _____ ☐ WPGC ☐ ORGANIZED ACTIVITY ☐ NON-ORGANIZED ACTIVITY

(5) IF ORGANIZED, NAME OF ACTIVITY: _____

(6) EXACT LOCATION WHERE ACCIDENT OCCURRED: _____

(7) WEATHER CONDITIONS _____

(8) CAUSE AND MANNER OF ACCIDENT: _____
_____
_____

(9) SPECIFIC NATURE AND EXTENT OF INJURIES: _____
_____
_____

(10) NAME OF INJURED _____ ☐ M ☐ F D.OB. _____ (MO) (DAY) (YR) AGE _____

STREET _____ CITY _____ PHONE # _____

(11) WITNESS # 1 _____

STREET _____ CITY _____ PHONE # _____

(12) WITNESS # 2 _____

STREET _____ CITY _____ PHONE # _____

(13) DID YOU WITNESS ACCIDENT? ☐ YES ☐ NO

(14) WAS FIRST AID ADMINISTERED? ☐ YES ☐ NO BY _____

(15) DESCRIBE FIRST AID ADMINISTERED. _____

(16) ASSISTANCE REQUESTED? ☐ YES ☐ NO ☐ POLICE ☐ FIRE ☐ AMBULANCE ☐ OTHER _____

(17) ASSISTANCE REQUESTED BY MEANS OF ☐ TELEPHONE ☐ RADIO ☐ PERSONAL CONTACT

(18) ASSISTANCE REQUESTED BY _____

(19) NAME OF OFFICER IN CHARGE _____ AGENCY _____

(20) REMOVED TO HOSPITAL? ☐ YES ☐ NO BY _____ TIME: ___:___ ___ M.

(21) NAME OF HOSPITAL? _____

(22) IF MINOR, PARENTS WERE CONTACTED AT _____:_____ ___ M.

PARENTS CONTACTED BY _____

NAME OF PERSON RECEIVING CALL _____

(23) WERE POLICE PHOTOS TAKEN? ☐ YES ☐ NO

(24) WAS PROPERTY DAMAGE INVOLVED ☐ YES ☐ NO

(25) EXTRA PAGES ATTACHED ☐ YES ☐ NO # OF PAGES _____

(26) OTHER REPORTS SUBMITTED? ☐ YES ☐ NO TYPES AND #s _____

(27) PERSON MAKING REPORT _____ TITLE _____
(SIGNATURE)

FOR OFFICE USE ONLY:

POLICE CONTACT MADE? ☐ YES ☐ NO DATE _____ (DAY) (MO) (DAY) (YR) BY _____

NAME OF INVESTIGATING OFFICER _____

POLICE REPORT #s _____

INSURANCE CONTACTED? ☐ YES ☐ NO DATE _____ (DAY) (MO) (DAY) (YR) BY _____

INFORMATION ATTACHED ☐ YES ☐ NO # OF PAGES _____

```
CHAMPAIGN PARK DISTRICT            General Manager
                                   Dtr. of Operations    _____
    PARTICIPANT ACCIDENT REPORT    Dtr. of Recreation    _____
                                   Safety Committee      _____
                                   File                  _____
                                                         _____

DATE OF ACCIDENT        /   /
                               A.M.
TIME OF ACCIDENT _____ P.M.

NAME OF INJURED _____ AGE _____ PHONE NUMBER _____

HOME ADDRESS _____

WHERE DID ACCIDENT OCCUR? _____

WHICH PARK OR FACILITY? _____

WHERE IN THE PARK OR FACILITY? _____

WHAT PART OF BODY WAS INJURED? _____

WHAT TYPE OF INJURY (E.G., BRUISE, LACERATION) WAS SUSTAINED? _____

DETAILS OF ACCIDENT _____

_____

WITNESS TO ACCIDENT _____

ADDRESS _____ PHONE NUMBER _____

STAFF MEMBER PRESENT _____

ACTION TAKEN:

    _____ A.  None required.
    _____ B.  Parent(s) called.
    _____ C.  First aid given.  Explanation _____
    _____ D.  Ambulance called.
    _____ E.  Injured taken to _____Hospital by _____

                                _____
                                Signature of person making report
- - - - - - - - - - - - - - - - - - - - - - - - - - - - - - - - - - - - - -
                             FOLLOW-UP

DATE  /   /    Done by _____

NOTES OR REMARKS _____

File a copy of this report in the administrative offices by no later than
5 p.m. the next working day.
```

PROCEDURES IN THE EVENT OF A SERIOUS INJURY

I. Emergency Process

   A. Give first aid.

   B. If it is determined that an ambulance is needed, contact the Fire Department through their emergency number, which is 344-2211. They are hooked into the ambulance service and can provide EMT service themselves. The following information must be given to them:

      1. Location and direction.
      2. Someone to meet them when they arrive.
      3. What happened.
      4. Victim's condition.
      5. Additional information after ambulance is dispatched.

   C. Call parent/guardian or person victim is staying with.

   D. Call victim's doctor, if known.

   E. Contact police at 687-5111 when documentation might be needed because of possible legal questions that may come up later.

   F. Fill out accident report.

II. If, after giving first aid, it is determined that an ambulance is not needed but transportation is still needed, the following procedures should be followed:

   A. Give first aid.

   B. Contact parent/guardian in the case of a youth, or relatives or neighbors if it is an adult, to see if they can transport the person to their home or to a medical facility or doctor, if needed.

   C. We do not want staff transporting people who have been injured, even if the injury is minor, in their own personal cars, or even in City vehicles, unless it is a last resort. The first method of transportation would be the ambulance if there is a need for that type of transportation. If the ambulance is not needed, the first method of transportation should be the victim's parents, relatives, or friends. The last resort would be our staff transporting either in our City vehicles or in their own vehicles.

   D. Staff person must fill out an accident report form, getting all details and information as needed.

In both cases, under Sections I and II, if there are police involved, they will make a complete report. Get those reports to the various places they need to go, but this does not excuse the staff person from the responsibility of filling out our departmental accident report and any other reports required by the situation.

SS:so/PR1a25

PARTICIPANT/VOLUNTEER ACCIDENT FORM

Eugene Parks & Recreation Department

Name of Injured Person _____ Age _____

Address_____ Phone _____

Date of Accident _____Time _____am _____pm

Place of Accident _____

Description of Accident _____

_____

Description of Injury _____

_____

Was First Aid Given? _____ By Whom? _____

What Type of First Aid Was Given? _____

_____

Signature of Person Making This Report (x)_____

For a MAJOR ACCIDENT, complete the following:

Was Injured Person Removed From the Scene of the Accident? _____

If Yes, To Where and By Whom (Name and Address? _____

_____

Names and Addresses of Witnesses _____

_____

_____

_____

_____

_____

Name of Person Notified (Parent or Guardian if Injured is a Minor) _____

_____

Eugene Parks & Recreation Department Staff Member Notified (Normally Your
Immediate Supervisor, Unless Instructed Otherwise) _____

Did Person Making the Report Witness the Accident? _____

Signature of Facility or Program Area Supervisor (X)_____

* *

ON THE BACK ARE PROCEDURES TO BE FOLLOWED IN THE EVENT OF A SERIOUS INJURY.

114

EMPLOYEE AND VOLUNTEER GUIDELINES FOR PATRON INJURIES OR ACCIDENTS

District policy requires that all reported accidents or injuries to patrons be given proper attention by employees. The following procedures should be followed insofar as they may apply to any particular situation:

1. Dial 911 for an ambulance in any case of severe bleeding, loss of consciousness, chest pain or any bleeding from the ears, nose or mouth after a head injury; or whenever the employee feels an ambulance may be needed. Injured persons often cannot judge the extent of their own injury.

2. First aid should be rendered within the ability of the employee to do so.

3. As soon as the situation has stabilized, record the name, address and date of birth of the injured person.

4. Record names and addresses of any witnesses and their account of the accident.

5. Make no response to questions or accusations concerning liability for the accident. Concentrate efforts on care of the injured person and gathering information.

6. Prepare an accident report form before completion of duty and leave with employee's supervisor.

FURNISHED BY: JOHNSON COUNTY PARK & RECREATION DISTRICT
SHAWNEE MISSION, KANSAS

APPENDIX E

EMERGENCY PROCEDURES

EMERGENCY MEDICAL AUTHORIZATION

City of Kettering Parks &
Recreation Dept.
_____

Child's Name
_____

Address
_____

Telephone
_____

Purpose - To enable parents and guardians to authorize the provision of emergency treatment for children who become ill or injured while under the City of Kettering Parks and Recreation Department's authority, when parents or guardians cannot be reached.

GRANT CONSENT

In the event reasonable attempts to contact me at _____ (phone number) or _____ (other parent or guardian) at _____ (phone number) have been unsuccessful, I hereby give my consent for: (1) the administration of any treatment deemed necessary by Dr. _____ (preferred physician) or Dr. _____ (preferred dentist), or in the event the designated preferred practitioner is not available, by another licensed physician or dentist: and (2) the transfer of the child to _____ (preferred hospital) or any hospital reasonably accessible.

_____
_____

This authorization does not cover major surgery unless the medical opinions of two other licensed physicians or dentists, concurring in the necessity for such surgery, are obtained prior to the performance of such surgery.

Facts concerning the child's medical history including allergies, medications being taken, and any physical impairments to which a physician should be alerted: _____

_____

_____

_____

_____

_____
Date

_____
Signature of Parent or Guardian

_____
Address

119

BUFFALO GROVE PARK DISTRICT
530 BERNARD DRIVE
BUFFALO GROVE, ILLINOIS 60089

EMERGENCY TREATMENT RELEASE FORM FOR MINORS

A minor may not be treated even in an emergency situation except when, in the opinion of the physician, a life is in the balance. The Buffalo Grove Park District requests that you sign and complete the bottom portion of this form so we can be prepared should medical help be deemed necessary and we cannot reach you.

EMERGENCY TREATMENT RELEASE

TO WHOM IT MAY CONCERN:

As a parent and/or guardian, I do herewith authorize the treatment by a qualified and licensed medical doctor of the following minor in the event of a medical emergency which, in the opinion of the attending physician, may endanger his or her life, cause disfigurement, physical impairment or undue discomfort if delayed. The authority is granted only after a reasonable effort has been made to reach me.

Name of Minor_____Relationship_____

Dates when Release is intended; December 2 - March 31, 1986

This release form is completed and signed of my own free will with the sole purpose of authorizing medical treatment under emergency circumstances in my absence.

Signed_____
                FATHER-MOTHER-LEGAL GUARDIAN

Address_____Phone_____

Family Physician_____Phone_____

Specific medical allergies, chronic illness or other conditions staff should be aware of:_____

_____

Other contact in case of emergency:

Name_____Relationship_____Phone_____

Please indicate whether your child is to be dismissed on his/her own or is to be picked up by checking the appropriate box:

          [   ] DISMISSED ON OWN   [   ] PICKED UP

Senior Transportation Program

Medical Emergency

In the event a rider experiences a cardiac or respiratory arrest or serious injury:

1. The van driver initiates immediate first aid treatment.

2. Call 911; give location of vehicle, your name, and statement about the medical emergency.

3. Call Senior Transportation Coordinator at

4. Give the paramedic or emergency medical technician on the emergency vehicle pertinent information explaining the incident and request them to contact the Senior Transportation Coordinator at   for further information.

5. Fill out the following information and return to the Senior Transportation Coordinator immediately.

_____

Name of Person Injured_____

Date of Incident_____ Time of Incident_____

Location_____

Description of Incident_____

_____

_____

Description of Action Taken_____

_____

_____

Witness: Name_____

          Address_____

          Name_____

          Address_____

Driver's Signature_____ Date_____

_____   _____
Senior Transportation Coordinator's Signature   Date

FURNISHED BY MAPLE GROVE, MN PARKS AND RECREATION BOARD

121

Senior Transportation Program

WHAT TO DO IN CASE OF AN ACCIDENT

1. Make sure your passengers are not injured, and give aid if necessary.

2. Make sure occupants of other vehicle are not injured.

3. Call an ambulance, if necessary.

4. Call the police, call the Senior Transportation Coordinator at

5. Make sure there are traffic controls out and move vehicle out of traffic, if possible.

6. Make NO statement except to Police.

7. Get information about other vehicle.

8. Give other driver information on bottom of this sheet.

9. Get names and addresses of any witnesses.

10. Fill out accident report when you get back to the office.

**********************INFORMATION NEEDED ON OTHER VEHICLE********************

Owner's Name_____ Address_____

Driver's Name_____ Address_____

Driver's License# _____ Phone#_____

Make of Car_____ Year_____ License#_____ Color_____

Name of Insurance Co._____ Amount of Damage_____

What Parts Damaged_____

Direction of Travel____ Speed_____ Did Driver Signal_____ Kind_____

Accident Happened at Street_____ City_____

Time_____ Date_____ Weather was_____ Road was_____

**********************TEAR OFF AND GIVE TO OTHER DRIVER**********************

My Name_____ Address_____

Driver's License#_____ Vehicle Owned By_____

Insured By_____ Bus #_____ License #_____

FURNISHED BY MAPLE GROVE, MN PARKS AND RECREATION BOARD

122

APPENDIX F
REPORTING DEVICES

SUN PRAIRIE PARKS AND RECREATION DEPARTMENT
VANDALISM REPORT

PARK _____ DATE DISCOVERED _____ TIME _____

DISCOVERED BY _____

WAS VANDALISM WITNESSED? _____

NAME OF INDIVIDUAL(S) IF WITNESSED _____ ADDRESS _____

_____ ADDRESS _____

CATEGORY TYPE OF DAMAGE (SEE CHART BELOW) _____
                                          NUMBER   TYPE

DESCRIBE DAMAGE DONE _____

_____

_____

ESTIMATED DATE AND/OR TIME OF DAMAGE: _____

_____

ESTIMATED DOLLAR AMOUNT OF DAMAGE _____

WERE POLICE NOTIFIED? _____ WHEN _____ TIME _____

WHO TOOK THE INFORMATION AT THE POLICE STATION: _____

SIGNED _____

CATEGORY TYPE OF DAMAGE DUE TO VANDALISM

1. BREAKAGE: Fracturing, shattering, smashing, or crushing apparatus,
    equipment or facilities, or parts thereof.

2. SURFACE GRAFFITI OR MARKING: Superficial writing or drawing on, or
    discoloring the surface of a wall, door, partition, panel, sign or other
    facility or apparatus.

3. DISFIGUREMENT: Scratching, cutting, denting, carving, gouging or
    pentrating through the surface, either exposing the undersurface or making
    a hole completely through the item.

4. DISASSEMBLY OR REMOVAL: Unfastening screws, bolts, nuts, nails or hinges
    to take apart a piece of equipment, apparatus or facility.

5. BURNS: Combustion, charring, scorching or singeing of flammable
    materials.

6. BLOCKAGE: Obstructing, plugging or stopping utility supply or waste
    lines.

7. VEGETATIVE DAMAGE OR LOSS: Breaking, chopping, burning, nailing, making
    ruts or removing trees, shrubbery, flowers, turf or groundcover.

125

CHAMPAIGN PARK DISTRICT

VANDALISM REPORT FORM

DATE _____19___

PLACE WHERE VANDALISM
OCCURRED _____

ITEM VANDALIZED _____

_____

TYPE OF VANDALISM _____

_____

APPARENT REASON FOR VANDALISM _____

_____

EXACT LOCATION _____

_____

TIME _____ a.m.   p.m.

ACTION TAKEN _____

_____

_____

APPROXIMATE COST TO REPAIR _____

PREVENTIVE MEASURES TAKEN _____

_____

_____

REPORTED BY _____

DATE OF REPORT _____

ADDITIONAL COMMENTS:

YOUR SIGNATURE _____

NILES PARK DISTRICT

UNSAFE CONDITION REPORT

SUBMITTED BY: _____ DATE: _____

LOCATION OF CONDITION: _____

DESCRIPTION: _____

_____

_____

_____

_____

_____

CORRECTED BY: _____ DATE: _____

COMMENTS (INCLUDE COSTS): _____

_____

_____

_____

_____

DEPT. HEAD SIGNATURE : _____ DATE: _____

1.   PERSON REPORTING CONDITION SHOULD FILE ORIGINAL FORM WITH
       MAUREEN McNICHOLAS.

2.   AFTER CONDITION HAS BEEN RECTIFIED, DEPARTMENT HEAD SHOULD
       SUBMIT ORIGINAL COMPLETED FORM TO MAUREEN McNICHOLAS.

NILES PARK DISTRICT
7877 Milwaukee Ave.
Niles, IL 60648

INCIDENT REPORT

AM
Date of Incident _____ Time of Incident _____PM

Exact Location of Incident _____

_____

Description of Incident   _____

_____

_____

_____

_____

Witness (other than employee) Name _____

Address _____

Phone _____

 Witness (other than employee) Name _____

Address _____

Phone _____

Employee Witnesses (please list) _____

_____

_____

Employee Filing Report_____

Date of Report _____

City of Cuyohoga Falls, Ohio Park & Recreation Department P.O. Box 361, Cuy. Falls, Ohio 923-9921, ext. 209 UNUSUAL INCIDENT REPORT	Vandalism ( ) Law Violation ( ) Discipline ( ) Accident ( ) Unusual Behavior ( ) Other _____ ( )

Nature of Incident

Names, Addresses & Phone numbers of Individuals Involved

How you handled the incident

Disposition of Incident

What action should be taken by Park & Recreation Dept. & any further comment.

	Refer to Police Department		Desire Conference on this subject		Refer to:
By:		Date:		Supervisor:	

DEPARTMENT OF PARKS AND RECREATION SECURITY/INCIDENT REPORT
(To be submitted to the Safety Office within 24 hours)

☐ Damage to City/County Property   ☐ Damage to Private/Personal Property

☐ Stolen City/County Property   ☐ Stolen Private/Personal Property

☐ Alarm Situation   ☐ Other_____
(Specify)

Date/Time of Incident: _____/_____/_____   _____:_____ AM - PM

Location (facility & address): _____

Description of Incident: _____

_____

_____

_____

Witnesses: _____ _____ _____
(name/address/
phone)   _____ _____ _____

Police Notified: Yes - No   Officer's Name: _____

Badge Number: _____   Case (CAD) Number: _____

Action Taken: _____

_____

Third Party Injury: Yes - No   Injury Reported: Yes - No

Owner of Property: _____

Address: _____ Phone H _____-_____ W _____-_____

Individual(s) Responsible (if known):   City Employee: Yes - No

Name 1: _____ Address: _____

Ins Carrier: _____ Phone H _____-_____ W _____-_____

Driver's License: _____ Plate #/state: _____

Vehicle Description (make/model/yr): _____

Name 2: _____ Address: _____

Ins Carrier: _____ Phone H _____-_____ W _____-_____

Driver's License: _____ Plate #/state: _____

Vehicle Description (yr/make/model): _____

Repair/Replacement Cost: _____,_____,_____ = _____
                         (materials) (equipment) (labor)   Total Cost

Date/Time of Report: _____/_____/_____   _____:_____ AM - PM

Name/Title of Reporting Person: _____

Recommendations for Resolving incident: _____

Date/Time Received in Safety Office: _____/_____/_____   _____:_____ AM - PM

9/4/86 aly

UMPIRE REPORT

UMPIRE'S NAME _____

DATE OF INCIDENT _____ PARK _____

PERSON FILING COMPLAINT _____

TEAM NAME _____

COMPLAINT: _____

_____

_____

_____

_____

RISK MANAGEMENT – INCIDENT REPORTING

RELEASE DATE: October 8, 1986
REPLACES ISSUED DATED:

DEPARTMENT RESPONSIBLE: Management Services

Policy

The Park District is concerned with the safety of and health of its citizens and employees. The purpose of the Risk Management/Incident Reporting Program is to minimize the chance of injury, expedite incident reporting and investigation and to comply with applicable laws governing such injuries.

General Information

Two flow charts, 1) Work Related Injuries Flow Chart and 2) Park User Accident Review Flow Chart, relate to the Risk Management/Incident Reporting Program are attached to this policy. They summarize the actions/steps to be taken in handling these incidents. Flow charts with specific names and telephonenumbers are available by contacting th Principle Secretary within the Department of Management Services. Flow charts are to be POSTED at all work reporting locations. Specific forms for reporting incidents have also been developed. These charts and forms follow the Situation/Procedures section below.

Procedures

The following outlines, by situation or type of incident, the reporting procedures that are to be followed. Additional information, forms or charts are available from the Personnel Assistant or the Management Services Principle Secretary, as applicable.

Situation	Reporting Procedures/Forms
Work related injury of Hennepin Parks employee (permanent or seasonal).	Please refer to the Work Related Injuries Flow Chart. Complete the "First Report of Injury" form following the attached instructions. Forward a copy to the Personnel Assistant .
On duty injury of Hennepin Parks volunteer. (Hennepin Parks provides accidental death and medical insurance coverage for volunteers on duty.)	Complete side one of the "Notice of Claim" form provided by the Hartford and forward to the Management Services Principal Secretary .
Park User Injury	Please refer to the Park User Accident Review Flow Chart for specific procedures relative to severity of accident. Complete the "Hennepin Parks Accident Report" form and forward to the Management Services Principal Secretary.
Off-Duty Hennepin Parks Employee/Volunteer	Injuries sustained on Hennepin Parks property should be reported using the "Hennepin Parks Accident Report" form prescribed for a park user injury. DO NOT USE "FIRST REPORT OF INJURY" OR "NOTICE OF CLAIM" FORMS.
Accidents involving Hennepin Parks vehicle or property	Contact the Management Services Principal Secretary for appropriate State of Minnesota and/or insurance company reporting forms.

SUBURBAN HENNEPIN REGIONAL PARK DISTRICT

Risk Management
Work Related Injuries Flow Chart

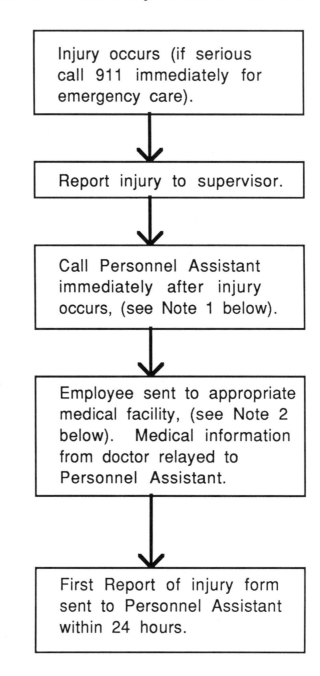

Injury occurs (if serious call 911 immediately for emergency care).

↓

Report injury to supervisor.

↓

Call Personnel Assistant immediately after injury occurs, (see Note 1 below).

↓

Employee sent to appropriate medical facility, (see Note 2 below). Medical information from doctor relayed to Personnel Assistant.

↓

First Report of injury form sent to Personnel Assistant within 24 hours.

Note 1: Injuries resulting in death, back injuries, broken limbs or other serious injuries are to be reported immediately to the Park District's Risk Manager.

Note 2: Current information as to the appropriate local clinic or medical facility is posted at all work locations

SUBURBAN HENNEPIN REGIONAL PARK DISTRICT

Risk Management
Park User Accident Review Flow Chart

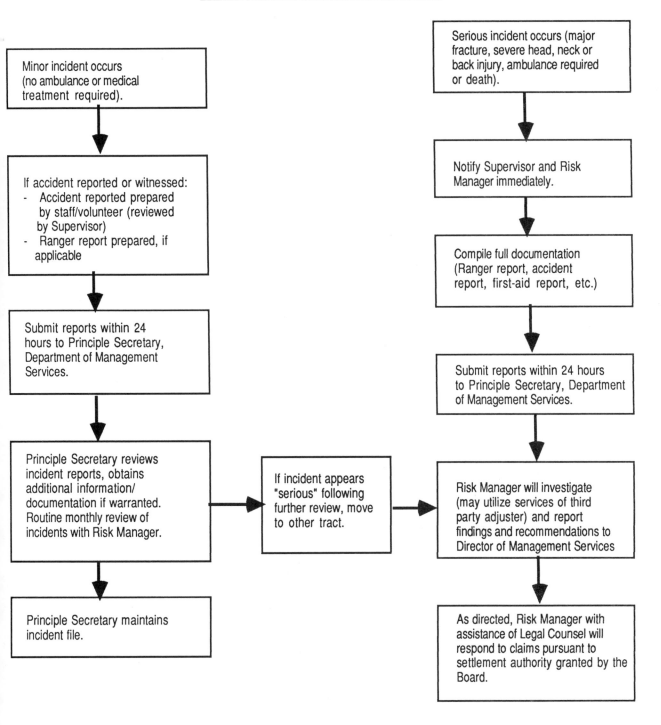

Note:

1) Once a claim is made process will immediately shift to "serious incident" tract - copies of claim and support documentation forwarded to Risk Manager .

2) Hyland Hills Ski Area accident reports will be prepared and maintained at the Ski Area with a copy of the summary sheet and reports submitted the Department of Management Services Principle Secretary. Incidents involving a death or multiple losses should be reported immediately to the Risk Manager, who in turn will investigate and serve as liaison to the insurance carrier.

APPENDIX G

INSPECTIONS

MIRACLE'S CHECK LIST

Location _____
_____
Date _____
Inspector _____

Fill in Equipment Type
(swing, slide, whirl, etc.)

EXAMINED CONDITION

												- Unrepairable
												- Jagged/exposed screws, bolts nuts
												- Jagged/ exposed concrete footings
												- Broken suppoorts/anchors
												- Broken rails, steps, rungs, seats
												- Loosebolts, nuts, etc.
												- Missing supports/anchors
												- Missing rails, steps, rungs, seats
												- Worn surgace material
												- Worn swing hangers or chain
												- Repainting necessary
												- Inadequate surfacing material under equipment
												- Worn bearings
												- Splintered wood
												- Wood checking
												- Lubricate moving parts
												- Other (specify)
												-
												-
												-

For More Copies of this Form Contact Your Local "Miracle Man", or write:

MIRACLE RECREATION
EQUIPMENT COMPANY
P.O. BOX 275
GRINNELL, IOWA 50112

Playground Inspection

Playgrounds in the Urbana Park District will be inspected by a member of the Facilities Maintenance staff weekly from April through October. The purpose of this weekly inspection is twofold: to insure that play areas are safe for play, and to maintain play features in a high state of repair. Electrical timers, photo cells, lights, and water fountains will also be checked to insure they are operational and that the lights are coming on at the desired time.

<u>Playgrounds will be inspected using a checklist and as follows:</u>

1. <u>Swings</u>: Insure chains are secure to swing seat and swing bar. S-hooks checked to insure they are closed and that chain cannot slip loose. Check pivot points/hinge fasteners for wear. Children's swings checked for same.

2. <u>Slides</u>: Surfaces are free from burrs, approaches/ladders are secure, adequate gravel/sand at base of slide.

3. <u>Merry-go-round</u>: Free moving, stable, hand holds are secure, surface around play feature is sand/pea gravel free of glass, metal or other sharp objects that might injure a user.

4. <u>Climbing bars</u>: All bars are secure, smooth, free of burrs. Surface underneath the play feature is free from glass, metal, other debris that might injure a user. Sand/pea gravel around and underneath play feature.

5. <u>Wooden Play Structure</u>: All walkways have boards secured. Any areas that are walked on, climbed on etc. have nails flush with surface. All fasteners have ends smoothed.

6. <u>Cable Slides</u>: Insure cable is secured properly with U-bolts. Pull for slide should be free to slide easily handle safe/secure.

7. Check for graffiti on play structures, use Vand-off to remove.

8. Water fountains will be checked for serviceability and vandalism.

9. Lights will be checked to insure they are working, coming on at the desired time and lenses are intact.

10. Timers for water play features, and all lights will be checked to insure they are functional and set for proper times.

11. Tennis courts - check nets and tie downs, replace/repair as necessary. Insure drains are open and courts are draining.

12. Ballfield - Backstop fencing check and repair, players "dug out" check and repair fencing and bench. Bleachers check and repair.

13. Restrooms will be checked to insure they are being cleaned, are functional, doors are working - hinges, locks, etc.

14. Park grills will be checked/repaired, insure they are being cleaned.

15. Basketball courts - check goals and nets replace/repair when necessary.

Any play features that are broken or unsafe and cannot be repaired immediately will be taken out of operation to insure nobody could be injured.

SUGGESTED PUBLIC PLAYGROUND MAINTENANCE CHECKLIST

Inspections should be conducted on a frequent, regularly scheduled basis. Following are some of the danger points that should be checked on each tour:

o Visible cracks, bending, warping, rusting, or breakage of any component.

o Deformation of open hooks, shackles, rings, links, etc.

o Worn swing hangers and chains.

o Missing, damaged, or loose swing seats; heavy seats with sharp edges or corners.

o Broken supports/anchors.

o Footings exposed, cracked, loose in ground.

o Accessible sharp edges or points.

o Exposed ends of tubing that should be covered by plugs or caps.

o Protruding bolt ends that do not have smooth finished caps and covers.

o Loose bolts, nuts, etc.

o Splintered, cracked or otherwise deteriorated wood.

o Lack of lubrication on moving parts.

o Worn bearings.

o Broken or missing rails, steps, rungs, seats.

o Surfacing material worn or scattered (in landing pits, etc.).
o Hard surfaces, especially under swings, slides, etc.

o Chipped or peeling paint.

o Vandalism (broken glass, trash, etc.).

o Pinch or crush points (exposed mechanisms, junctures of moving components, e.g., axis of seesaw).

o Tripping hazards such as roots, rocks or other environmental obstacles.

o Poor drainage areas.

SUGGESTED PUBLIC PLAYGROUND LEADER'S CHECKLIST

o Prepare written guidelines for playground operation, defining goals and procedures.

o Insist on first aid and accident training for playground leaders.

o Provide for constant supervision by establishing a written schedule.

o Instruct children and playground supervisors on how to use equipment. (Playground equipment safety should be taught in the classroom.)

o Conduct daily cleaning and check for broken glass and other litter.

o Do not permit children to use wet or damaged equipment.

o Do not permit too many children on the same piece of equipment at the same time; suggest that children take turns, or direct their attention toward other equipment or activities.

o Constantly observe play patterns to note possible hazards and suggest appropriate equipment or usage changes.

o Make periodic checkups, and request that worn or damaged pieces of equipment be replaced.

o Prepare written accident reports with special attention to surface conditions, type and extent of injury, age and sex of child, how the accident occurred, and weather conditions.

FROM: A Handbook for Public Playground Safety, Vol. 1: General Guidelines for New and Existing Playgrounds, U.S. Consumer Product Safety Commission, Wash. D.C.

PARK: _____   DATE: _____

INSPECTED BY: _____

	SATISFACTORY	UNSATISFACTORY	URGENT REPAIR REQUIRED	COMMENTS
1. Swings: Chains				
Hooks				
Seat				
Swivel Bracket & Bolts				
Lube				
2. Cable Slide: Cable				
Rope				
Pulley				
Nuts & Bolts				
3. Structures: Boards Secure/Wear-n-Tear				
Railing & Fences				
Ladders & Steps				
Slides				
Rollers				
Tire Swing				
Merry-Go-Round				
Miscellaneous				
4. Misc. Equipment: Nuts & Bolts				
Springs				
Fasteners				
Boards & Seats				
Material Under Structure				
5. Play Areas/Open Space: Contours				
Obstacles				
Lighting				
Obstructions				
Walkways				
Paths				
Handicap				
Fitness Trail				
Fitness Equipment				
6. Park Furniture: Boards				
Nuts & Bolts				
Frame & Braces				
7. Courts: Tennis				
Basketball				
Pickleball				
8. Parking Lots: Lighting				
9. Other (i.e., picnic tables, park signs)				
_____				
_____				
_____				

* * * * * * * * *   FOR OFFICE USE ONLY   * * * * * * * * *

Date Received by Supervisor: _____ Priority Work Scheduled: _____

Follow-Up Inspection Date: _____ By: _____

SUGGESTED PUBLIC PLAYGROUND PLANNERS' AND INSTALLERS' CHECKLIST

o Separation of equipment for different age groups.

o Placement of swing(s) or swing sets away from other activities or equipment.

o Adequate space for children to exit equipment such as slides or merry-go-rounds.

o Layout designed to promote a safe flow of traffic between areas.

o Fencing or other barriers to separate the playground from adjacent streets.

o Clearly marked "danger" zones (e.g., those areas covered by swinging seats from swing sets and areas in front of sliding boards).

o No equipment installed over hard surfaces such as concrete or asphalt.

o Accessible components of equipment adjacent to sliding surfaces shaped so that a child's clothing cannot be caught as the child uses the slides.

o No component or group of components forming angles or openings that could trap a child's head or any part of a child's body.

o Protective barriers on surfaces which are elevated more than 30 inches from an underlying surface, assuring that the barriers do not create another hazard (i.e., horizontal cross pieces on which children can climb).

o Handgripping components of size and shape to make them easy for a child to grasp.

o Climbing and gripping surfaces which are slip resistant under both wet and dry conditions.

o Explanation signs where needed, e.g., in color coded areas.

FROM: A Handbook for Public Playground Safety, Vol. 1: General Guidelines for New and Existing Playgrounds, U.S. Consumer Product Safety Commission, Wash. D.C.

MONTHLY COMMUNITY CENTER INSPECTION

DATE_____ CENTER_____

INSPECTED BY_____

C.C. SUPERVISOR_____

TIME:_____ A.M._____ P.M.

A - Ideal
B - Acceptable
C - Needs Improvement
D - Unacceptable

FLOORS	A	B	C	D	REMARKS:
Tile					
Carpet					
Gym					
REST ROOMS	A	B	C	D	REMARKS:
Clean					
Sanitized					
Stools					
Urinals					
Basins					
Mirrors					
Dispensers					
GEN. BLDG.	A	B	C	D	REMARKS:
Windows					
Sinks					
Counters					
Reg/Vents					
Walls					
Entrances					
Lights					
Storage					
Waste Cont.					
OUTSIDE	A	B	C	D	REMARKS:
Lawns					
Shrub Beds					
Pkg. Lots					
Garb. Area					

COMMENTS:

PARK MAINTENANCE CHECKLIST
Form #001

Date_____

Time_____

Park Name_____

Employee Name_____

                                                    Yes   No

1) Presence of downed tree limbs or potentially   _____   _____
   dangerous situations (if yes, correct the
   situation or note the location)   _____

2) Presence of damaged playground equipment   _____   _____
   (if yes, remove or note location)
                                            _____

3) Presence of damaged tables,benches or signs   _____   _____
   (if yes, note location)
                                            _____

4) Presence of erosion problems or damaged turf   _____   _____
   (if yes, note location)
                                            _____

5) Presence of chuckholes or damaged concrete   _____   _____
   (if yes, note location)
                                            _____

6) Presence of damaged or defaced barrels   _____   _____
   (if yes, note location)
                                            _____

7) Presence of glass or debris on parking lots   _____   _____
   or on hard-court surfaces
   (if yes, take necessary steps to   _____
   correct the situation)

8) Miscellaneous problems_____
_____
_____

Additional comments_____
_____
_____
_____

****
*   INFORMATION FROM THIS FORM SHOULD BE PHONED IN TO THE APPROPRIATE SECTION *
*   AS SOON AS POSSIBLE   *
*   (Land Improvements, Facility Maintenance, Forestry, etc.)   *
****

American Red Cross

Location _____

Inspected by _____   Date _____

	Yes	No
1. OSHA log maintained.	___	___
2. Floors, stairs, and handrails maintained in good repair.	___	___
3. Aisles, stairways, and doorways maintained free of obstructions.	___	___
4. Handrails provided for steps and stairs (four or more steps).	___	___
5. Permanent aisles and passageways appropriately defined.	___	___
6. Telephone, electrical, and extension cords guarded when crossing aisleways and walkways.	___	___
7. Filing and storage cabinets and wall lockers properly anchored and weights properly distributed to prevent tipping of units.	___	___
8. Tops of lockers, filing cabinets, cases, and other relatively high objects free of material.	___	___
9. Furniture and equipment positioned so there are no protruding parts to endanger employees.	___	___
10. Oily waste or rags and similar combustibles stored in covered metal containers.	___	___
11. Blades of electrical fans adequately guarded.	___	___
12. Telephone numbers of fire department and ambulances conspicuously posted.	___	___
13. Adequately trained personnel available and first aid supplies provided for emergency use.	___	___
14. Illumination meets recognized lighting standards.	___	___
15. Paint, plaster, and floor covering in good repair.	___	___
16. Inspections conducted at proper intervals on boilers.	___	___
17. Current safety posters displayed.	___	___

	Yes	No
18. Exits maintained free of obstructions.	___	___
19. Exit signs provided for exits.	___	___
20. Fire extinguishers are proper type and adequate number provided.	___	___
21. Extinguishers inspected monthly and annually.	___	___
22. Extinguishers hydrostatically tested at proper intervals.	___	___
23. Extinguishers placed where readily accessible (not blocked) and visible from several different directions.	___	___
24. Extinguishers mounted at proper heights.	___	___
25. Automatic sprinkler systems maintained and checked.	___	___
26. Flammable liquids stored in safety containers and the contents of each container identified.	___	___
27. Designated "NO SMOKING" areas strictly enforced.	___	___
28. Ash trays provided in authorized smoking areas.	___	___
29. Electrical circuits utilized effectively without creating overloads.	___	___
30. Noncurrent-carrying metal parts of cord and plug connected, and fixed equipment grounded.	___	___
31. Flexible cord used in approved manner—not substituted for fixed wiring where run through walls, doors, and openings—and attached to building surfaces or concealed.	___	___
32. Extension cords and plugs in good condition.	___	___
33. Conditions of walks, outside steps, driveways, parking surfaces, and so on, properly maintained.	___	___
34. Rugs and carpets secured and arranged to prevent slipping.	___	___

Unresolved Items From Previous Inspection:

A. Item # _____   Abatement Date _____

B. Item # _____   Abatement Date _____

C. Item # _____   Abatement Date _____

D. Item # _____   Abatement Date _____

American Red Cross Form 6506 (5-86)

APPENDIX H

OCCUPATIONAL SAFETY AND HEALTH ADMINISTRATION (OSHA)

OSHA's Purpose

Under the Act, the Occupational Safety and Health Administration (OSHA)was created within the Department of Labor to:

o Encourage employers and employees to reduce workplace hazards and to implement new or improve existing safety and health programs;

o Provide for research in occupational safety and health to develop innovative ways of dealing with occupational safety and health problems;

o Establish "separate but dependent responsibilities and rights" for employers and employees for the achivement of better safety and health conditions;

o Maintain a reporting and recordkeeping system to monitor job-related injuries and illnesses;

o Establish training programs to increase the number and conpetence of occupational safety and health personnel;

o Develop mandatory job safety and health standards and enforce them effectively; and

o Provide for the development, analysis, evaluation and approval of state occupational safety and health programs.

While OSHA continually reviews and redefines specific standards and practices, its basic purposes remain constant. OSHA strives to implement its Congressional mandate fully and firmly with fairness to all concerned. In all its procedures, from standards development through implementation and enforcement, OSHA guarantees employers and employees the right to be fully informed, to participate actively and to appeal actions.

The Act's Coverage

In general, coverage of the Act extends to all employers and their employees in the 50 states, the District of Columbia, Puerto Rico, and all other territories under Federal Government jurisdiction. Coverage is provided either directly by federal OSHA or through an OSHA - approved state program (see section on OSHA-Approved State Programs, p. 33).

As defined by the ACT, an employer is any "person engaged in a business affecting commerce who has employees, but does not include the United States or any State or political subdivision of a State." Therefore, the Act applies to employers and employees in such varied fields as manufacturing, construction, longshoring, agriculture, law and medicine, charity and disaster relief, organized labor and private education. Such coverage includes religious groups to the extent that they employ workers for secular purposes.

The following are not covered under the Act:

o Self-employed persons;

o Farms at which only immediate members of the farm employer's family are employed; and

o Workplaces already protected by other federal agencies under other federal statutes.

But even when another federal agency is authorized to regulate safety and health working conditions in a particular industry, if it does not do so in specific areas, then OSHA standards apply.

As OSHA develops effective safety health standards of its own, standards issued under the following laws administered by the Department of Labor are superseded: the Walsh -Healey Act, the Service Contract Act, the Construction Safety Act, the Arts and Humanities Act and the Longshoremen's and Harbor Workers' Compensation Act.

Services Available

Consultation Assistance

Free consultation assistance is available to employers who want help in establishing and maintaining a safe and healthful workplace. Largely funded by the Occupational Safety and Health Adminstration, the service is provided at no cost to the employer.

No penalties are proposed or citations issued for hazards identified by the consultant.

Confidential in nature, the service is provided to the employer with the assurance that his or her name and firm and any information about the workplace will not be routinely reported to OSHA inspection staff.

Exemption from OSHA general schedule inspections may be granted to eligible employers who meet certain requirements. Inspection exemption through consultation offers special recognition to employers who voluntarily take the initiative to make their workplaces safe and healthful.

Besides helping employers to identify and correct specific hazards, consultation can include assistance in developing and implementing effective workplace safety and health programs with emphasis on the prevention of worker injuries and illnesses. Training and education services are also provided, as well as limited assistance away from the worksite.

Primarily targeted for smaller employees with more hazardous operations, the consultation service is delivered by state government agencies or universities employing professional safety consultants and health consultants. When delivered at the worksite, consultation assistance includes an opening conference with the employer to explain the ground rules for consultation, a walk through the workplace to identify any specific hazards and to examine those aspects of the employer's safety and health program which relate to the scope of the visit, and a closing conference followed by a written report to the employer of the consultant's findings and recommendations.

This process begins with the employer's request for consultation and the commitment to correct any serious job safety and health hazards identified by the consultant. Possible violations of OSHA standards will not be reported to OSHA enforcement staff unless the employer fails or refuses to eliminate or control worker exposure to any identified serious hazard or imminent danger situation. In such unusual circumstances, OSHA may investigate and begin enforcement action.

Employers who receive a comprehensive consultation visit, correct all identified hazards, and demonstrate that an effective safety and health program is in operation may be excempted from OSHA general schedule enforcement inspections (not complaint or accident investigations) for a period of one year. Comprehensive consultation assistance includes an appraisal of all mechanical, physical work practices, and environmental hazards of the workplace and all aspects of the employer's present job safety and health program.

Additional information concerning consultation assistance, including a directory of OSHA-funded consultation projects, can be obtained by requesting OSHA publication No. 3047, "Consultation Services for the Employer."

U.S. Department of Labor
Occupational Safety and Health Administration
Regional Offices

Region I
(CT*, MA, ME, NH, RI, VT*)
16-18 North Street
1 Dock Square Building
4th Floor
Boston, MA 02109
Telephone (617) 223-6710

Region II
(NJ, NY*, Puerto Rico*, Virgin
Islands*)
1 Astor Plaza, Room 3445
1515 Broadway
New York, NY 10036
Telephone: (212) 944-3432

Region III
(DC, DE, MD*, PA, VA*, WV)
Gateway Building, Suite 2100
3535 Market Street
Philadelphia, PA 19104
Telephone (215) 596-1201

Region IV
(AL, FL, GA, KY*, MS, NC*, SC*, TN*)
1375 Peachtree Street, N.E.
Suite 587
Atlanta, GA 30367
Telephone (404) 881-3573

Region V
(IL, IN*, MI*, MN*, OH, WI)
230 South Dearborn Street
32nd Floor, Room 3244
Chicago, IL 60604
Telephone (312) 353-2220

Region VIII
(CO, MT, ND, SD, UT*, WY*)
Federal Building, Room 1554
1961 Stout Street
Denver, CO 80209
Telephone: (303) 844-3061

Region IX
(American Samoa, AZ*, CA*, Guam,
HI*, NV*, Pacific Trust Territories)
PO Box 36017
450 Golden Gate Avenue
San Francisco, CA 94102
Telephone (415) 556-7260

Region X
(AK*, ID, OR*, WA*)
Federal Office Building
Room 6003
909 First Avenue
Seattle, WA 98174
Telephone (206) 442-5930

Region VI
(AR, LA, NM*, OK, TX)
525 Griffin Square Building, Room 602
Dallas, TX 75202
Telephone (214) 767-4731

Region VII
(IA*, KS, MO, NE)
911 Walnut Street, Room 406
Kansas City, MO 64106
Telephone (816) 374-5861

*These states and territories operate their own OSHA approved job safety and health programs (except Connecticut and New York whose plans cover public employees only).

APPENDIX I
SUPERVISORY EVALUATION

CITY OF EUGENE, OREGON
PARKS & RECREATION DEPARTMENT
SUPERVISORY EVALUATION

EMP. No. _____   DEPT. _____   DIV. _____

☐ SCHEDULED
☐ UNSCHEDULED
☐ PROBATIONARY

EMPLOYEE _____

Date employed by City _____   Starting date this class _____

PRESENT CLASS TITLE _____

PRESENT RANGE _____ PRESENT STEP _____

PROPOSED CLASS TITLE _____

PROPOSED RANGE _____ PROPOSED STEP _____ DATE _____

SECTION A	a Exceeds Standards	b Meets requirements	c Needs Improvement	d Unacceptable	FACTOR CHECK LIST IMMEDIATE SUPERVISOR MUST CHECK EACH FACTOR IN THE APPROPRIATE COLUMN	e Does Not Apply
					1. Observance of scheduled work hours	
					2. Compliance with established policies	
					3. Safety practices	
					4. Works cooperatively w/other staff	
					5. Relates to & communicates w/public	
					6. Understands responsibilities & functions	
					7. Accepts responsibility	
					8. Work judgments	
					9. Planning and organizing	
					10. Meeting deadlines	
					11. Quality of work	
					12. Effective time management	
					13. Accepts direction	
					14. Adaptability to change (flexibility)	
					15. Effectiveness under stress	
					16. Operation & care of equipment	
					17. Initiative	
					18. Energy and enthusiasm	
					19. Understanding of overall organization	
					20.	
					21.	
					22.	
					23.	

FOR EMPLOYEES WHO SUPERVISE OTHERS

					24. Training and instructing	
					25. Evaluating	
					26. Scheduling and coordinating	
					27. Productivity, quality of work	
					28. Supervisory control	
					29. Leadership	
					30. Operational economy	
					31. Judgments and decisions	
					32. Fairness and impartiality	
					33. Safety record	

SECTION B Record job STRENGTHS AND DEFICIENCIES
Record job STRENGTHS and superior performance incidents, and/or DEFICIENCIES or job behavior requiring improvement or correction. (Explain checks in columns C & D.)

SECTION C Record PROGRESS ACHIEVED in attaining previously set goals for improved work performance for personal, or job qualifications.

SECTION D Record specific GOALS or IMPROVEMENT PROGRAMS to be undertaken during next evaluation period.

SUMMARY EVALUATION - Check Overall Performance

1 ☐ Exceeds Standards   3 ☐ Requires Improvement

2 ☐ Effective - meets standards   4 ☐ Not Satisfactory

Rater: I certify this report represents my best judgment
☐ I DO ☐ I DO NOT recommend this employee be granted permanent status. (Final report only)

☐ I DO ☐ I DO NOT recommend a Merit Pay increase for this employee. (Where applicable)

Rated by: _____ Date: _____
Reviewed by: _____ Date: _____
Employee: I certify that a copy of this report has been given to me. I understand my signature does not necessarily indicate agreement.

Comments: (May be attached)
Employee Signature: _____ Date: _____

SOURCES OF ADDITIONAL INFORMATION ON ESTABLISHING RISK MANAGEMENT PROGRAMS

Government officials seeking further information on risk management could contact the following organizations.

Risk and Insurance Management Society, Incorporated (RIMS)
205 East 42nd Street
New York, New York   10017
Phone (212) 557-3210

RIMS is a national organization with over 2,000 corporations, institutions, and governmental bodies in the United States and Canada and includes 83 per cent of the Fortune 500 list. The Society functions as a clearinghouse for information on risk management and sound insurance procurement practices.

PRIMA (The Public Risk and Insurance Management Association)
1140 Connecticut Avenue, NW
Suite 210
Washington, DC   20036
Phone (202) 828-3614

PRIMA is exclusively devoted to the risk management and insurance concerns of the public sector entities. PRIMA publishes a monthly newsletter, sponsors workshops, seminars, conferences, and training programs and holds an annual conference in the spring of each year.

Public Agency Risk Managers Association (PARMA)
Insurance and Risk Manager
County of Santa Clara
County Service Center
1555 Berger Drive, Bldg. 2
San Jose, CA   95112

PARMA is composed of 110 municipalities, school districts, and utilities in California. The purpose of this organization is to consider, discuss, and exchange ideas for the improvement and functioning of the risk management of governmental agencies. PARMA holds monthly meetings, except during the summer.